AF658847

Silkworm Crop Protection
Concepts and Approaches

"An Ounce of Prevention is Worth a Pound of Cure"

Silkworm Crop Protection
Concepts and Approaches

Dr. Mohammad Ashraf Khan
Director
Central Sericultural Research & Training Institute
Central Silk Board, Ministry of Textiles
Govt. of India, Pampore
(Jammu & Kashmir)

Madan Mohan Bhat
Scientist–D
Regional Sericultural Research Station
Central Silk Board, Ministry of Textiles
Govt. of India, Sahaspur
Dehradun (Uttarakhand)

Dr. Tribhuwan Singh
Scientist–C
Research Extension Centre
Central Silk Board, Ministry of Textiles
Govt. of India, Rampur Road
Una (Himachal Pradesh)

2026
Daya Publishing House®
A Division of
Astral International Pvt. Ltd.
New Delhi – 110 002

© 2021, AUTHORS
First Published, 2011
Reprinted, 2026

ISBN: 978-81-7035-717-9 (Hardbound)
ISBN: 978-93-5124-184-3 (International Edition)

Publisher's note:

Every possible effort has been made to ensure that the information contained in this book is accurate at the time of going to press, and the publisher and author cannot accept responsibility for any errors or omissions, however caused. No responsibility for loss or damage occasioned to any person acting, or refraining from action, as a result of the material in this publication can be accepted by the editor, the publisher or the author. The Publisher is not associated with any product or vendor mentioned in the book. The contents of this work are intended to further general scientific research, understanding and discussion only. Readers should consult with a specialist where appropriate.

Every effort has been made to trace the owners of copyright material used in this book, if any. The author and the publisher will be grateful for any omission brought to their notice for acknowledgement in the future editions of the book.

All Rights reserved under International Copyright Conventions. No part of this publication may be reproduced, stored in a retrieval system, or transmitted in any form or by any means, electronic, mechanical, photocopying, recording or otherwise without the prior written consent of the publisher and the copyright owner.

Published by : **Daya Publishing House®**
A Division of
Astral International Pvt. Ltd.
– ISO 9001:2015 Certified Company –
4736/23, Ansari Road, Darya Ganj
New Delhi-110 002
Ph. 011-43549197, 23278134
E-mail: info@astralint.com
Website: www.astralint.com

Digitally Printed at : **Replika Press Pvt. Ltd.**

Preface

One of the unique contributions of the biology to mankind is the discovery of silk popularly known as the 'Queen of Textiles'. It is a proteinacious material 'par excellence' secreted by the lepidopteron sericigenous insect silkworm, *Bombyx mori* (L.) which feeds on mulberry leaves (*Morus* sp.). The discovery of natural relationship between the two has led an idea of production of silk in systematic manner. In order to produce more and more silk, efforts have been made to exploit the relationship between the two to its logical end. As a result of this, many countries ventured to take-up the task by developing suitable methods and technologies leading to the birth of sericulture industry.

Different components such as mulberry cultivation for production of quality mulberry leaves as a source of food for silkworm, improved method of silkworm rearing technology for healthy growth and development of larvae, silkworm egg production technology to maintain productivity and quality besides processing and reeling of cocoons have been well defined. As a result, country experienced a quantum jump in silk production and India has emerged as the second largest producer of silk in the world. In recent times, cocoon production has been considered as an important cash crop from the status of a very traditional and small subsidiary crop of marginal returns. Thanks are due to the pioneering efforts of Indian sericulture scientists to improve productivity per unit area. In fact, sericulture industry in India has been making steady and sustained progress through planned approaches. The current improvement in productivity and quality has made Indian sericulture highly attractive to the farmers.

The silkworms are susceptible to various diseases and attacked by pests and parasites. The diseases and pests together cause considerable damage to the silk industry. It has been proven that one silkworm disease 'pebrine' can destroy entire silk industry of a country. The outbreak of silkworm pest 'Uzi fly' can cause even more than 10–30 per cent loss to cocoon production. These threats imposed by pests and diseases necessitate extreme care in handling the silkworm. In general, outbreak of diseases and pests causing continuous crop failure has been usual phenomenon associated with tropical sericulture. But when innumerable changes are taking place in the society, sericulture scientists cannot remain as a silent spectator and therefore studied their causal agents, symptoms, pathogenesis, mode and source of infection, predisposing factors, epidemiology, biology, management, prevention and control and published the results here and there in different forms. However, there is no updated compendium of information in sericulture which provides extensive and comprehensive coverage on these aspects and various strategies to be adopted for their prevention and control as well as their occurrence.

Therefore, it was thought desirable to publish a comprehensive book on the subject. This book is designed to address wide range of readers, experts, university teachers, students, researchers, technologists, policy makers and to fulfill the hopes and aspirations of all those engaged in sericulture. It will serve as a very useful guide and will motivate and assist in the efforts to find solutions to the existing problems in order to prevent and control the diseases and pests of silkworm to increase production, productivity and quality. It is very well established that 'an ounce of prevention is worth a pound of cure' and it may be three or more pounds true in management of silkworm diseases and pests. This book has many unique features. It comprises diseases of silkworm *viz.*, infectious (bacterial, fungal, viral and protozoan) and non-infectious (arthropod diseases, poisoning, physiological ailments) and their occurrence, pathogen and disease cycle, prevention and control measures; pests of silkworm *viz.*, Uzi fly, dermestid beetles, mites, birds, rodents etc. and its taxonomic position, distribution, biology, life span, prevention as well as control measures to achieve sustained and quality cocoons with increase production and productivity. Also included are forewarning and forecasting of pests and diseases to contain them before they cause any damage. The information furnished in this book will be of immense importance not only to Indian sericulture but also to South Asian and African countries and will find an application at all levels of sericulture.

To present the comprehensive and updated information in this book *"Silkworm Crop Protection–Concepts and Approaches"*, we have drawn necessary information, photographs and scores from published books, documents, periodicals, journals, technical reports etc. and help taken from all of them is gratefully acknowledged.

It is with great pleasure, we wish to express our sincere thanks to all those we had interactions and enlightened discussion which stimulated and prompted us to take up this onerous task of compiling all the available information on the pests and diseases of mulberry silkworm. We wish to place on records our profound thanks to all those friends and well wishers who have directly or indirectly helped in one way or the other and for the constant encouragement in bringing out this publication. A reliable guide and lovable compilation, this book is sure to appeal all those associated directly or indirectly with sericulture industry.

We profoundly thank Sri Anil Mittal, Publisher, Daya Publishing House, New Delhi whose interest and enthusiasm have brought out this book with an excellent presentation within a short period.

All-out efforts have been made to incorporate correct and authentic information in the present book. Nevertheless, we accept all the responsibility for any omission or deficiency that might have crept inadvertently, in despite of our best efforts and intensions, please bring out such errors to the notice of the authors and publishers. The views and suggestions from users of this book are welcome to improve upon future editions.

Mohammad Ashraf Khan
Madan Mohan Bhat
Tribhuwan Singh

Contents

Chapter 1
Introduction

Sericulture in India has been a powerful tool for rural employment and poverty alleviation, as every acre of irrigated mulberry garden can provide full time employment to as many as 13 persons throughout the year. Silk being an exclusive fibre and popularly as "Queen of Textiles", the money moves from the rich and urban market to the poor and rural producers. As the developed countries retreating from the silk production in view of increased cost of human power, silk production provides hopes and opportunities to the developing countries. Having realized the benefits of investing resources in sericulture, the Union Government and the States over the years have laid emphasis on programmes based on sericulture for rural development. The role of sericulture and silk manufacturing industry in putting the country in its present position in the global scenario and the potential that exists for the agrarian economy like India, to further lead the world silk market owing to its rich diversity in respect of agro-climatic zones, diversity in the variety of silk that no single country can boast of, skilled manpower that creates magic out of this queen of textiles cannot be overlooked by any planner.

India enjoys the unique distinction of being the only country in the world to produce all the four commercial varieties of silk–Mulberry, Tasar, Eri and Muga and is the second largest producer of silk next only to China and has been recording consistent growth in the production and productivity. As India encompasses wide geographical and agro-climatic variations, mulberry sericulture is distributed in temperate, sub-tropical and tropical regions, while the major share comes from the tropics.

Among several factors, which influence the seed cocoon yield as well as commercial cocoon yield and quality, silkworm diseases and the insect and non-insect pests form an important component. The mulberry silkworm is attacked by insects such as tachinid parasitoids, dermestid beetles, ants, earwigs etc. The pests and parasites other than insects are mite, nematode, wall-lizards, rats, squirrels and birds that are also known to inflict considerable damage to silkworm and its crops.

The mulberry silkworm, *Bombyx mori* (L.), like any other insect, is prone to various diseases occurring in nature. Having been domesticated over centuries, it developed total dependence on man who has to take care of it. During its growth, the silkworm comes in contact with various pathogens and under the influence of the environment, the pathogen's capability to infect and its own capability to resist or succumb or co-exist, infection occurs. When the physiological equilibrium of the host is lost with the interference of the pathogen, a disease is said to occur. It has been proven that one silkworm disease 'pebrine' can destroy entire silk industry of a country. This threat imposed by silkworm diseases necessitates extreme care in their handling. It is very well established that there is no practical way available for curing infected larvae. Therefore, precaution, identification and strong disinfections are the only methods available for preventing diseases. In general, outbreak of diseases during silkworm rearing and sometimes continuous crop failure has been usual phenomenon associated with tropical sericulture. The threat of the disease is associated with the factors like poor quality of mulberry leaf, unfavorable weather conditions, lack of independent rearing houses for effective disinfections, poor hygiene and above all faulty rearing practices.

It is necessary to familiarize one-self with the principles underlying the initiation, development and spread of silkworm diseases, to identify, prevent or cure to obtain a stable cocoon yield. In small and short-lived insects, it is difficult to treat and cure the disease besides which shall also be uneconomical. It is very well established that 'an ounce of prevention is worth a pound of cure' and it may be three or more pounds true in the management of silkworm diseases and pests. Prevention is therefore suggested for containing silkworm diseases. Each disease is caused by a specific pathogen known as an etiological agent. The causes include biological, chemical, nutritional and environmental factors. The biological factors causing diseases are viruses (Nuclear polyhedrosis, Cytoplasmic polyhedrosis, Infectious flacherie and Densonucleosis), bacteria (Bacterial septicaemia, Bacterial toxicosis and Bacterial diseases of digestive tract), fungi (White

Muscardine, Green Muscardine, Black Muscardine, Brown Muscardine and Aspergillosis), protozoa (Pebrine) and arthropods; all of which are parasites; and all excepting arthropods are infectious. Agro-chemicals, pyrethroids, exhaust gases from automobiles and factories, smoke, residue from disinfectants, etc. are among the chemical agents causing diseases. The chemical agents are non-parasitic and non-infectious. Physical agents include mechanical injury during silkworm rearing, feeding, spacing, mounting, sex separation of larvae/cocoons etc. Severe injury sometimes leads to instantaneous death, whereas mild injury weakens the larvae.

Of these diseases, pebrine is one of the most serious maladies, which determines success or failure of sericulture industry in any country. This is evidenced by the historical fact that the rise and fall of pebrine disease corresponds with the ups and downs of sericulture industry in silk producing countries of the world. Although several years of research has highlighted certain preventive measures for major silkworm diseases, the occurrence is on very high scale in India causing considerable loss not only to seed cocoon crop but also to commercial crop every year.

A number of reviews, handbooks and bulletins are available to describe pests and diseases of mulberry silkworm on certain specific lines or as a part of book chapters. However, these are inadequate to reflect pests and diseases properly in order to enrich the knowledge of sericulturists, students, researches and scientists etc. besides policy makers to take appropriate decision and strategies to contain and prevent it.

This book therefore, provides comprehensive details of pests and diseases of mulberry silkworm and their management written to cater to the specific needs of Indian States. This publication aims at serving the basic needs of sericulturists *i.e*, production of healthy silkworm crop for harvesting better quality silk. This as a reference book will be of immense help to the students and teachers of sericulture; to the scientists working in labs and in the field; to the sericulture extension workers and for general academic/professional interest. Attempts have been made to:

☆ Discuss the major and minor pests of silkworm found in Indian States, their systematic position, distribution, pest status, seasonal incidence and nature of damage, biology and management approaches.

☆ Discuss the major and minor diseases of silkworm found in Indian States, their seasonal incidence, symptoms, pathogen and diseases cycle and management approaches.

☆ Discuss on disinfection and hygiene.

☆ Discuss on the strategies and approaches of forewarning and forecasting of silkworm pests and diseases.

Chapter 2
Silkworm Pests

Among several factors, which influence the cocoon yield of silkworm seed as well as commercial cocoon production, silkworm diseases and the insect and non-insect pests form an important component. The mulberry silkworm, *Bombyx mori* is attacked by insects such as tachinid parasitoids, dermestid beetles, ants, earwigs etc (Narayanaswamy and Devaiah, 1999). The pests and parasites other than insects are mites, nematodes, wall-lizards, rats, squirrels and birds that are also known to inflict considerable damage to silkworm and its crops. Major pests infecting mulberry silkworm (*Bombyx mori*) in India and other countries are presented in Table 2.1.

[1] Major Pest

Uzi Fly

Among the insect pests of mulberry silkworm, the Uzi fly, *Exorista bombycis* (Louis) (*Exorista sorbillans* Wiedmann)

Table 2.1: Pests of mulberry silkworm

Sl.No.	*Pests*	*Country*	*Incidence*
1	**Uzi fly**		
	Exorista bombycis	Bangladesh, China,	Throughout the
	Exorista sorbillans	Japan, India, Korea,	year
	Exorista myiasis	Thailand and Vietnam	
	Crossocosmia sericariae	Japan	Seasonal
2	**Dermestid beetle**		
	Dermestes sp.	India and Japan	Throughout the year
3	**Himefly**		
	Ctenophorocera pavida	Japan	Seasonal
4	**Mite**		
	Pediculoides ventricosus	China, India and Japan	Seasonal
5	**Hair caterpillar**		
	Euproctis similes	China and Japan	Seasonal
	Setora postornata		

is a primary larval endo-parasitoid of the silkworm, *Bombyx mori*. It is distributed in silk producing countries *viz.*, China, India, Japan, Korea, Thailand, Sri Lanka, Burma, Bangladesh, Vietnam etc. The other three commercially reared silkworms namely tasar, muga and eri are also reported to be parasitized by this fly. There are more than 55 alternate hosts recorded for this fly in nature but mulberry silkworm (*Bombyx mori)* is most preferred host. The extent of damage ranges from 10–30 per cent.

Systematic Position

Phylum	:	Arthropoda
Class	:	Insecta
Order	:	Diptera
Family	:	Tachinidae
Sub family	:	Goniinae
Tribe	:	Exoristini
Genus	:	*Exorista*
Species	:	*bombycis* (Louis)

Synonyms

- ☆ *Oestrus bombycis* (Louis)
- ☆ *Trycolyga bombycum* (Becher)
- ☆ *Trycolyga bombycis* (Louis)
- ☆ *Tricholyga bombycis* (Becher)
- ☆ *Oestroea bengalensis*
- ☆ *Tricholyga bombycum*
- ☆ *Tricholyga sorbillans* (Wiedemann)
- ☆ *Thrycolyga sorbillans* (Wiedemann)
- ☆ *Tachina sorbillans* (Wiedemann)
- ☆ *Tricholyga* (or *Thrycolyga*) *sorbillans* (Wiedemann)
- ☆ *Exorista sorbillans* (Wiedemann)
- ☆ *Exorista bombycis* (Louis)

Distribution

Exorista bombycis has been reported prevalent in Burma, China, Thailand, Sri Lanka, Japan, Korea, India and other South East Asian countries. The fly is reported for the first time to cause heavy damage to silkworm crops from southern parts of India, which was totally free from the damage of fly pest (Jolly and Kumar, 1985).

Biology

There are four distinct stages in the life cycle of the Uzi fly *viz.*, egg, maggot, pupa and adult. The period of different stages of growth varied according to temperature, season and time of incidence during the year. The fly is considerably larger than a housefly and is blackish gray in colour (Datta and Mukherjee, 1978a) with four prominent longitudinal black strips on the thoracic region and three crosswise broad bands on the abdomen. The abdomen is conical. Male fly is generally larger than female with a body length of about 12 mm in male and 10 mm in female. Wing span is about 10 mm and wings are covered with dark grey hairs. Lateral regions of the abdomen are covered with bristles, which are denser in male than in female and restricted mostly to last two abdominal segments in the latter. Pulvilli are broad in male than in female. Eyes are chocolate brown and antennae blackish brown in colour. Proboscis and mouth parts are well developed. The life span of adult fly varies with *sex* and season. Males survive for about 5–15 days while female lives for 20–25 days (Patil and Govindan, 1984a). Survival is least during summer seasons. The differences between male and female flies are:

- ☆ Males are generally larger (12 mm) than the females (10 mm).
- ☆ Five bristles on the head region in male, whereas three such bristles in females.
- ☆ Four longitudinal lines on the dorsum of thorax of the male are more prominent than in female.

- ✰ Pulvilli (legs) of males are larger than in females.
- ✰ Width of frons of male is narrower than that of female.
- ✰ Lateral regions of the abdomen are covered with bristles, which are denser in male than in female.
- ✰ Males have external genetalia covered with brownish orange hairs on the ventral side of the abdominal top.

The adult Uzi flies attain sexual maturity in 1.5–2.0 days after emergence. In nature, these flies copulate in air, live on nectar of flowers, and honeydew excreted from aphids and scale insects. The adults are polygamous. They mate 1–2 times within 24 hrs of adult emergence. They can mate 3–7 times during the adult life. In nature, mating duration ranges from half an hour to two and half hours. Oviposition starts approximately 2 days after emergence. A single mated female fly can lay about 300–1000 eggs in its life span during different seasons prevailing in India with an overall average of 500–600 eggs. Usually 2–3 eggs are laid on each larva and the oviposition continues until death. The fly prefers later stages of silkworm for egg laying. The ventral side and inter-segmental regions are the most preferred sites for egg laying. Eggs are small, oblong, elongated oval or bean shaped, creamy white in color, which measures about 0.45–0.56 mm in length and 0.25–0.30 mm in width. The ventral surface of egg is flat and membranous and is in close contact with the host skin (Datta and Mukherjee, 1978a; Thangavelu and Sahu, 1986). Depending on the season egg hatches in 2–5 days after oviposition and tiny maggots enter the body of the larva by making a perforation on the integument leaving its shell outside. At the point of penetration the parasitized silkworm larva shows a characteristic black scar. The marking alone is sufficient for the diagnosis of Uzi fly infestation.

The maggot is fusiform, creamy whitish and measures 1.4–1.7 cm in length and 0.3–0.5 cm in width with a pair of pharyngeal hooks at the anterior end and passes through three instars within the body of the host. The first two instars are yellowish white in color while third instars maggots are creamy white. Maggots have 11 body segments. They feed on fat bodies, leaving silk glands and lives for 4–6 days inside the body of the silkworms. Full-grown maggot cuts the integument of host with pharyngeal hooks leading to the death of the host. After coming out from the body of the host, maggots crawl in search of cracks and crevices, soil or darker regions where it forms puparium. Before pupation, it becomes motionless and the body shrinks. The pupal period lasts for 10–12 days. Pupae are oblong and light reddish brown to dark reddish brown in color. Males emerge earlier than females. The fly completes 10–14 generations in a year in tropical regions. In temperate regions it complete 6–7 generations while in arctic regions they hardy complete 4–5 generations. The duration of life cycle is inversely related to the temperatures and directly proportional to relative humidity (Narayanaswamy *et al.*, 1993b).

Life Span

Longevity of adult fly varied with sex and season. Females survive longer than the males in any given season. However, a pronounced seasonal variation in the longevity of both the males and females are recorded (Kumar, 1987). The survival duration for a female is always a very important and decisive factor in controlling the species as an effective parasitoid, especially so when the female parasitoid has the potential to lay the eggs till the last day of its survival. Both the sexes' exhibits shorter life span during summer compared to other seasons. Females survive for about 12 days during summer compared to 17–18 days in other seasons. Males during summer survive for about 10 days, whereas it survives for 16–17 days during other seasons.

Adult Uzi Fly Depositing Eggs on Silkworm Body

Mating Behaviour

The adult fly attains sexual maturity in 1.5–2.0 days after emergence. Repeated mating is more common (up to 8 times) and both polygamy and polyandry are observed. Mating occurs 2–3 times in 24 hrs (Datta and Mukherjee, 1978a; Jolly, 1982; Narayanaswamy and Devaiah, 1994 & 1998). Mating generally takes place during early morning or in the late evening.

Flight Range

The knowledge of flight range is an important factor and plays a key role in formulating pest management strategies. Narayanaswamy *et al.* (1994a & b) reported 2.7 km flight range of Uzi fly.

Period of Occurrence

The pest occurs throughout the year in tropical countries. The maximum infestation takes place during rainy season followed by winter and least in summer (Kumar, 1987). However, its incidence is higher from August to September.

Extent of Damage

From the point of view of monetary loss, the techinid species that attacks the silkworm larvae are unquestionably the most harmful members of the family Tachinidae. It causes considerable damage to silkworm crops ranging from 10–30 per cent. The maximum infestation takes place during rainy season followed by winter and least in summer (Kumar, 1987) and the incidence of this fly pest is very high in tropical sericultural region compared to temperate regions.

Symptoms and Nature of Damage

At the initial stage of infestation minute creamy white oval eggs smaller than pinhead are observed on the skin of the larvae. Infestation of this fly in 3rd, 4th and early 5th instar results in death of larvae before they reach to spinning stage. When parasitization occurs in late 5th instar, the mature maggot comes out by piercing the cocoons and thereby rendering the cocoons unsuitable for reeling. Infested silkworm larvae or pupae can be identified by the presence

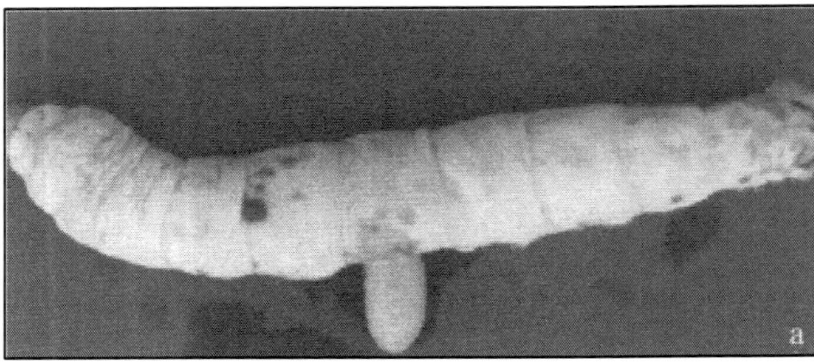

Uzi Fly Maggot Emerging from Affected Silkworm Body

of black scar on the skin, where the maggot penetrates into the body of host larvae. Bivoltine cocoon shells are compact and stiff, therefore, if its larvae are parasitized in late 5th instar, maggots fail to come out and hence pupate inside the cocoon and the flies die inside the cocoon. It causes considerable damage to silkworm crops in India. Krishnaswami *et al.* (1964) reported seasonal damage of

Uzi Pierced Silkworm Cocoons

silkworm crops due to this parasitoid infestation in West Bengal exceeding 40 per cent.

Host Range

Besides *Bombyx mori*, 95 species of insects belonging to 20 families of Lepidoptera and one family of Hymenoptera are known to be parasitized by *E. bombycis* worldwide (Narayanaswamy and Devaiah, 1999). However, its life cycle is reported to be completed successfully only on *Achoea janata, Antheraea assamensis, A. mylitta, Helicoverpa armigera, Samia ricini, Spilosoma obliqua* and *Spodoptera litura.* Host species of Uzi fly and reporting countries is presented in Table 2.2.

Table 2.2: Host Species of Uzi Fly and Reporting Countries

Host Species	*Reporting Countries*
Acherontia sp. (Sphingidae)	Ceylon
Acherontia lachesis (Sphingidae)	India and Ceylon
Andraca bipunctata (Bombycidae)	India and Ceylon
Attacus ricini (Saturniidae)	India and Ceylon
Bombyx mori (Bombycidae)	India, Ceylon, Japan, Korea
Cosmotriche divia (Lasiocampidae)	India
Dasychira mendosa (Lymantridae)	India, Ceylon, Malaysia
Dasychira thwaitest (Lymantridae)	India, Ceylon
Heliothis armigera (Noctuidae)	India, South Africa
Lymantria beatrix (Lymantridae)	Malaysia
Lymantria dispar (Lymantridae)	China
Metanastria hyrtaca (Lasiocampidae)	Ceylon, India, Malaya
Taragama dorsalis (Lasiocampidae)	India
Perina nuda (Lymantridae)	India
Thiacidas postica (Lymantridae)	Ceylon, India
Setora nitens (Limacodidae)	Malaysia

Contd...

Table 2.2–Contd...

Host Species	*Reporting Countries*
Saturnia spini and *S. pyri* (Saturniidae)	Europe
Arcta caja (Arctiidae)	Europe
Bombyx mandarina (Bombycidae)	China
Amathusia phidippus (Amathusidae)	Malaya
Attacus ricini Boisd. (Saturniidae)	Ceylon, India, Java
Cephonodes hylas (Sphingidae)	Malaysia
Hasora alexis (Hesperidae)	Ceylon
Laelia suffuse (Lymantridae)	Malaysia, Czechoslovakia
Lymantria monacha (Lymantridae)	Czechoslovakia
Metanastria sp. (Lasiocampidae)	India
Nygmia phaeorrhoea (Lymantridae)	Europe
Saturnia pavonica (Saturniidae)	Europe
Philosamia walkeri advena (Saturniidae)	Malaysia

Management of Uzi Fly

Since Uzi fly has many alternate hosts in nature, it cannot be eradicated instead it can only be managed. Beside prevention and control following strategies should be taken into consideration for management of Uzi fly.

(*i*) Exclusion Method

- ☆ Use Uzi fly proof wire mesh or nylon nets on doors, windows and ventilators, which should be kept closed (Jolly *et al.*, 1982). A significant reduction in Uzi infestation has been reported by employing this method (Kumar *et al.*, 1986b). Moreover, this method is suitable for independent type of rearing houses.

- ☆ Antechamber must be attached to each rearing house to prevent entry of Uzi fly in the rearing apartment at the time when workers enter in.
- ☆ Use nylon net on the individual rearing trays for preventing the fly from getting access to the silkworm for oviposition is also reported (Siddappaji and Channavasavanna, 1981; Kotikal *et al.*, 1989). Covering of the individual rearing stands with fly proof wire mesh (Kumar, 1987) is also reported which prevents ovipositing female Uzi fly to accesses silkworm larvae.
- ☆ Transportation of only healthy cocoons to new seed producing regions of the country to prevent Uzi flies entry into these areas.

(*ii*) Cultural/Mechanical Method

- ☆ Pick Uzi infested silkworm larvae and emerging maggots in rearing trays and kill them. Further, collection of maggots and pupae of Uzi fly from cocoon markets, grainages and rearing establishments and their destruction by burning or by dipping them in 0.5 per cent soap solution.
- ☆ Make floor of rearing rooms/houses, cocoon markets and grainages establishments free from cracks and crevices to avoid pupation of maggots at unnoticed places.
- ☆ Uzi infested larvae spin cocoons earlier a day or two. Such cocoons should be harvested separately and stifled.
- ☆ Simultaneous skipping of silkworm rearing by all the farmers in a locality helps in non-availability of silkworms for continuous multiplication.

- ☆ Maggots falling from mountages should be collected and destroyed.
- ☆ Sorting out of Uzi pierced cocoons before transportation to cocoon markets helps in preventing further spreading of Uzi maggots besides fetching higher price for the good cocoon, which is free from Uzi infestation.
- ☆ Placing the mountages indoors at the time of spinning so that Uzi maggots coming out from the Uzi infested spinning larvae can easily be collected and destroyed.
- ☆ Avoid transportation of seed cocoons from Uzi infested areas to uninfected areas.
- ☆ Use of levigated China clay to prevent Uzi flies to lay eggs on the silkworm.

(*iii*) Physical Method

- ☆ Use light-cum-sticky trap to attract adult flies and get caught on the sticky board (Devaiah and Patil, 1986).
- ☆ Use of kerosene water trap near doors and windows to attract and kill ovipositing adults (Jolly *et al.*, 1982).
- ☆ Use of fishmeal trap outside the rearing room to trap adult flies.
- ☆ Use of food bait trap–an agar based food attractant has been formulated by mixing jaggery, D. maltose, citral, vanillin and weak formaldehyde to attract and kill the adults of Uzi fly. The attractant is placed in the silkworm rearing houses and the effectiveness of the bait in attracting both the sexes

of Uzi fly is found to be as high as 90 per cent (Singhamony *et al.*, 1990).

(*iv*) Chemical Method

- ☆ Use of commercial formulation of Uzicide or Uzi-powder in the rearing house.
- ☆ Diflubenzuron in low concentration (100 ppm) has been reported to have ovicidal activity and is used to kill the eggs of Uzi fly.
- ☆ Use of 2 per cent bleaching powder solution as ovicide for effective control (Bhattacharya *et al.*, 1993; Kumar *et al.*, 1995).

Uzi Trap

Uzi trap is a chemo-trap formulated from the mixture of indigenous chemical, which does not contain any insecticide and is available in the form of tablet. The chemical is cost effective and environmental friendly in nature. It is a kind of trap used for attracting the adults. Dissolve one tablet of Uzi trap in one liter of water. The solution prepared should be kept in light coloured flat trays and placed near the windows both inside and outside at the height of the base of the window. The solution should be used from 3rd instars onwards till spinning. When solution becomes dirty due to accumulation of dust, dead insects, silkworm litter etc., it should be discarded and fresh solution should be prepared for further use. Uzi trap solution is safe to silkworms, pets and to human beings. It is very simple to adopt. It can be used along with other control strategies of Uzi fly in IPM. One packet of Uzi trap containing 12 tablets is sufficient for use in rearing of 100 Dfls.

Uzicide

It is a liquid ovicidal formulation of benzoic acid which is sprayed on the body of the silkworm larvae in each instar from 3rd stage onward on alternate days except the period of moulting. The formulation has been developed with the view to kill the eggs of Uzi fly (Kumar *et al.*, 1987). It is sprayed on the 2nd and 4th day of IV instar and 2nd, 4th and 6th days of V instars. Silkworm should be given feeding half an hour after spraying. Four to five liters of uzicide is required for spraying on larvae of 100 Dfls. Uzicide kills the eggs when it is sprayed on the Uzi infested silkworms, resulting in non-emergence of Uzi maggots from the eggs. Spraying of uzicide can be performed with any ordinary hand sprayer. Field studies at farmers' level have demonstrated suppression of 93 per cent Uzi incidence. The application of uzicide has no adverse effects on the silkworm rearing performance and also on the persons associated with it.

Uzi Powder

It is an ovicidal dust formulation, which kills the Uzi eggs when dusted on the body of the silkworms. Dusting is carried out from III instars onwards. Uzi powder should be taken in a muslin cloth and dusted uniformly after bed cleaning. Silkworm should be fed half an hour after dusting. Four to five kilogram of Uzi powder is required for dusting on 100 Dfls larvae. The Uzi powder is dusted @ 3 gm per sq. ft. of silkworm bed starting from 2nd day of III instar on every alternate day till initiation of spinning. The powder is not dusted when the silkworms are under moult. Uzi powder should be kept out of the reach of the children. Bed disinfectant should not be applied when Uzi powder is dusted. Uzi powder contaminated silkworm litter should not be fed to the cattle and facemask should be used while dusting the Uzi powder.

Levigated China Clay

Mature silkworm larvae mounted on chandrike (mountages), and kept in open space for spinning are liable for attack of Uzi fly. Hence, dusting of China clay over the spinning larvae and mountages is effective to reduce the Uzi fly infestation during spinning period. Finely powdered levigated China clay should be dusted through muslin cloth over the spinning larvae and chandrike. It is to be dusted @ 3 gm/100 spinning larvae (before mounting on chandrike) and also @ 4 gm/sq. ft. area of bamboo chandrike before mounting.

Bleaching Powder Solution

Two percent bleaching powder solution is reported effective in killing the egg stage of Uzi fly. When sprayed on the body of the silkworm, starting from 2nd day of III instar through initiation of spinning (except during moult) on alternate day after bed cleaning, the Uzi infestation is reduced considerably. Bleaching powder solution (2 per cent) is also reported to act as a degumming agent by whom the eggs of Uzi get detached from the silkworm body when they come in contact with the solution. Ten liters of the solution is required for spraying during rearing of 100 Dfls larvae of silkworm.

(*v*) Biological Method

Biological control of the pests is the most safe and eco-friendly approach in pest management strategy. In biological control, natural enemies of the pest concern those having high searching ability, synchronomous with host life, host specificity, and adaptations to field conditions, easy rearing and multiplication methods are preferred (Devanathan *et al.*, 1982).

Table 2.3: Natural Parasitoids of Uzi Fly

Sl.No.	*Parasitoids*	*Family**	*Nature of Parasitoid***
1.	*Brachymeria intermedia*	Chalcididae	Solitary pupal
2.	*Brachymeria lugubris*	Chalcididae	Solitary pupal
3.	*Dirhinus anthracia*	Chalcididae	Solitary pupal
4.	*Dirhinus himalayanus*	Chalcididae	Solitary pupal
5.	*Exoristobia philippinensis*	Encyrtidae	Gregarious pupal
6.	*Marmoniella vitripennis*	Chalcididae	Solitary pupal
7.	*Nesolynx dipterae*	Eulophidae	Gregarious pupal
8.	*Nesolynx thymus*	Eulophidae	Gregarious pupal
9.	*Pachycrepoideus veeranai*	Pteromalidae	Solitary pupal
10.	*Pachycrepoideus vindimmae*	Pteromalidae	Solitary pupal
11.	*Pleurotropis* sp.	Pteromalidae	Solitary pupal
12.	*Spalangia cameroni*	Eulophidae	Solitary pupal
13.	*Spalangia endues*	Diapriidae	Gregarious larval
14.	*Tetrasticus howardii*	Eulophidae	Gregarious larval
15.	*Trichopriya khandalus*	Diapriidae	Gregarious larval
16.	*Trichospilus diaptraeae*	Chalcididae	Gregarious larval
17.	*Brachymeria* sp.	Chalcididae	Solitary pupal
18.	*Dirhinus* sp.	Chalcididae	Solitary pupal
19.	*Trichopriya* sp.	Diapriidae	Gregarious pupal

*: Order–Hymenoptera; **: Endoparasitoid.

Natural parasitoids *viz.*, *Nesolynx thymus, N. dipterae, Trichopria, Exoristobia phillipinensis, Dirhinus anthracia* etc.

has been identified to control Uzi fly (Kumar *et al.*, 1989; 1993a & b). So far, 20 larval/pupal parasitoids are known (Table 2.3).

Among this *N. thymus* is the most popular biological control agents of Uzi fly today, because of its high reproductive rate and higher female ratio. One lakh adult females should be released in three doses corresponding to IV and V instars and within one or two days after cocoon harvest at 8000, 16,000 and 76,000 adults respectively. Parasitoids should be released immediately after sunset in the rearing houses, places of mountage storage, near mountages with spinning larvae and also near the manure pits. However, its host searching ability and parasitization potential has kept it on the top of the other parasitoids (Table 2.4).

Table 2.4: Searching Ability and Parasitization Potential of Parasitoids of Uzi Fly

Parasitoids	*Searching Ability (distance in feet)*	*Parasitization Range (per cent)*
Nesolynx thymus	200	33 – 94
Exoristobia phillippinensis	90	0 – 9
Trichopriya sp.	90	0 – 3
Dirhinus sp.	200	0 – 66

An IPM package comprising of an ovicide (Uzicide) against eggs, augmentation/insinuative release of indigenous gregarious *N. thymus* and solitary *Dirhinus* sp. parasitoids against pupae and dusting of dimilin on maggots/puparia to suppress the reproductive efficiency of adults has been recommended. In IPM, biological control coupled with mechanical control (nets) has been most successful.

Quantity requirement of items in chemical and biological methods is presented in Table 2.5.

Table 2.5: Quantity Requirement of Chemical and Biological Items

Item	*Quantity*	*Unit Rate (Rs.)*	*Amount (Rs.)*
Uzi trap	1 packet	10.00	10.00
Uzicide	4.5 liters	15.00	67.50
Uzi powder	4.5 kg.	20.00	90.00
N. thymus	1 lakh adults	20.00	20.00
Total expenditure (without Uzi powder)			97.50
Total expenditure (without uzicide)			120.00

(*vi*) Induction of Sterility

Sterilization of male and female can be achieved through exposing the maggots and puparia to gamma rays or treatment of maggots; pupae and adult with chemosterilents, which affects their reproductive potential (Kumar *et al.*, 1990). Tepa, Thiotepa, Penfluron and Diflubenzuron chemosterilent is known to bring sterility in Uzi fly besides affecting eclosion, longevity, mating, competitiveness and fecundity (Datta and Mukherjee, 1978b; Kumar, 1987). Semiochemicals (pheromones and allelochemicals) (Kasturibai *et al.*, 1986; Persoons *et al.*, 1993), essential oils (lemon, lime and orange), aqueous extracts of plant products (Eucalyptus oil) and quarantine measures are also useful to control Uzi fly.

(*vii*) Quarantine Measures

Quarantine measures in pest management are suggested with the objective of preventing the migration of the pest from one region of the country to the other or from one country to another (Channabasavanna *et al.*, 1993). The Uzi fly is an accidentally introduced pest in the state of Karnataka. The pest has found its way into this major silk producing state through pest-infested cocoons brought from Eastern region of the country. Hence, to restrict such pest introduction to new areas, it has been suggested that only eggs of silkworm need to be supplied to the new areas instead of transporting seed cocoons for preparation of silkworm eggs (Govindan *et al.*, 1998).

(*viii*) Plant Products

Plant products are one of the important weapons available for insect control. Plant products have high biological activity, narrow or intermediate specificity, low or negligible mammalian toxicity, short persistence in the environment and effective in low concentrations (Narayanaswamy and Devaiah, 1999). The plant isolates affect developmental stages including eggs, fully grown larvae, nymphs or maggots, pre-pupae and female adults. Attempts have been made in the past to evaluate plant products as ovicides, larvicides, pupicides, oviposition deterrents/repellants against Uzi fly (Berman *et al.*, 1990; Narayanaswamy and Devaiah, 1998).

(*ix*) Integrated Pest Management (IPM)

For effective suppression of Uzi infestation, an IPM package comprising of an ovicide (uzicide–a liquid formulation of 1 per cent Benzoic acid) against eggs and augmenting release of the indigenous gregarious (*N. thymus*) and solitary (*Dirhinus* sp.) parasitoids against pupa and dusting of Dimilin on maggot/puparia to suppress the reproduction efficiency of adults has been developed (Kumar *et al.*, 1991). A simplified IPM package consisting of spray of uzicide and release of only *N. thymus* parasitoids has also been suggested (Kumar *et al.*, 1993a) and tested which yielded desirable result. Uzi trap as one of the component of IPM package has been suggested (Kumar *et al.*, 1996) to contain Uzi infestation effectively. However, the combination consisting of uzicide, uzitrap and *N. thymus* has been found to be best in containing Uzi incidence below economic injury level. Use of IPM package against Uzi fly has been found as the best approach in terms of eco-friendliness, higher level of pest suppression and optimization of cocoon production.

[2] Minor Pests

Mulberry silkworm is also attacked by several other insect species *viz.*, Coleoperans (*Alphitobiulaevigatus, Lyprops cuticollis, Necrobie rufipes, Tribolium castaeneum*) and many species of Dermestes; *Dermapteran labia arachidis*; Tachinids *Crossocosmia zebina* and *Ctenophorocera pavida* and Acarid, *Pediculoids ventricosus*. As these pests cause occasional damage and therefore are considered of minor economic importance.

(*a*) Dermestid Beetles

Dermestes belong to the order Coleoptera; super family Demestoidea and family Dermestidae. They damage pupae and adults in the grainages in general and stored cocoons in particular. Five species of dermestid beetles *Dermestes alter, D. cadsvarinus, D. vulpinus, Attagenus fasiatus* and *Anthrenus verbesci* have been reported to attack the cocoons of *Bombyx mori* (Sengupta *et al.*, 1990).

Seasonal Occurrence

Presence of pest has been reported throughout the year and almost in all the sericultural zones of the country.

Biology

Adults of *Dermestes alter* are light yellow in color which changes to dark brown or black and measures approximately 7 mm in body length. Female starts egg laying 5 days after emergence. They lay 150–250 eggs in the floss of the cocoons. The eggs are milky white, elongate and measures 1.90 x 0.48 mm in size. The eggs hatch in 5–7 days after oviposition. Newly hatched grubs are white in colour, 2.4 mm in length; spindle shaped and covered with hairs. These grubs turn to black from second instars onwards. The grubs undergo 4–6 moults. The total life span of grub is 27–28 days after which it pupates. Pupal period is approximately 7–8 days after which emergence of adult takes place. The total life cycle of the beetle takes about six weeks.

Dermestes cadverinus adults are dark brown in colour, 10 mm in length with oval elongated body and club shaped antennae. The eggs are oval, 2 mm in size and milky-white in colour, which hatches in about 7 days. Newly hatched grubs are spindle shaped reddish brown in colour, covered with hairs. They start feeding on dried animal matter. The insect prefers to live in darker places. It moults 5–6 times in 4–8 weeks and become pupa. The larvae and adults are attracted by the smell of stifled cocoons and dried pupae inside. They bore into the cocoon and eat the dried pupae and thus damage cocoons making them unfit for reeling.

Adults of *Dermestes vulpinus* are shiny reddish brown to black in colour, subparallel in shape covered with dense hairs. This is a cosmopolitan species and is commonly known as hide beetle. The males are slightly smaller than females, bear a pit and a brush of hair on the fourth sternite and the four short basal tarsal segments of fore and mid legs lack the fine golden testaceous hair and also do not form ventral pads. Adult females lay eggs in batches of two or three, sometimes singly and oviposition is favored under high humid conditions at 25–30°C temperature. The number of eggs laid by the adult varies from 200–850. Eggs are white in color and cylindrical in shape. Hatching takes place from the eggs after 2–4 days of oviposition. Depending on the temperature, humidity and kind of food, they moult 7–14 times and the larval period varies from 25–60 days. Full-grown larva is dark brown with a medium yellow stripe dorsally and is densely covered with hairs. They pupate in the last larval skin and the adult emerges from the pupa in

Silkworm Cocoons Damaged by Dermestid Beetle

5–8 days. There may be 3–6 generations in a year depending on the temperature, humidity and other climatic conditions.

Symptoms and Nature of Damage

Grubs and adults make hole in the cocoon, enter inside and eat the dried pupae. They also damage pierced and melted cocoons. It is also observed that they sometimes attack ovipositing adults of silkworm in the grainages and the damage is caused mostly on the abdominal region. The damage level estimated by Thiagarajan and Govindaiah (1987) due to the beetle attack to the pupae of silkworm is 16.62 per cent and moth 3.57 per cent with total loss of 20.19 per cent in Government grainages in Karnataka.

Management

- ☆ Avoid longer storage of rejected/pierced cocoons and rejected layings.
- ☆ Collect the grubs and adults either by sweeping or using a vacuum cleaner and destroy them by burning or dipping in soap water.
- ☆ Proper disinfections of grainage premises, rearing house and cocoon storage room besides periodical cleaning.
- ☆ Provide a wire mesh to the doors and windows of pierced cocoon storage rooms and grainage rooms to avoid entry of the beetles and grubs.
- ☆ Pierced cocoon storage room should invariable be constructed away from the grainage building.
- ☆ Dip wooden articles of the storage room and of the grainage building in 0.2 per cent Malathion solution for 2–3 minutes. Safe period for the use of appliances is 10 days after thoroughly washing with water and sun drying for 2–3 days.

☆ Fumigate dried cocoon (not live) storage room with Methyl bromide at 0.5 gm per $3m^2$ for 3 days.

☆ Pierced cocoons should be stored in Deltamethrin treated bags (soak the bags in 0.028 per cent deltamethrin solution and dry in shade).

☆ Spray 0.028 per cent Deltamethrin solution on walls and floor of pierced cocoon (PC) storage room once in three months.

☆ Sprinkle bleaching powder (200 gm/m^2) all around inner wall of PC storage room to prevent crawling of grubs from PC room.

Table 2.6: A Tentative World List of Dermestid Insect Pests of Stored Silkworm Cocoons and their Products (Vijay Veer *et al.*, 1996)

Species	*Commodity Damaged*	*Country*
Thylodrius contractus	Silk fabrics	USA
Dermestes alter	Cocoons, Raw silk	Germany, India, USA, Japan
Dermestes coarctatus	Eggs, Cocoons, Silk	Japan
Dermestes frischii	Cocoons, raw silk	Italy, Central Asia
Dermestes lardarius	Cocoons, Eggs, Caterpillars	Bulgaria, France, Italy
Dermestes leechi	Cocoons	India
Dermestes maculates	Moth, Raw silk	Italy, India
Dermestes murinus	Cocoons, Raw silk	Italy
Dermestes peruvianus	Raw silk	Britain
Dermestes tesclataocollis	Raw silk	India
Dermestes undulates	Cocoons, Raw silk	Central Asia, India
Dermestes vorax	Cocoons, Raw silk	India
Attagenus fasciatus	Cocoons, Fabrics	India
Attagenus birmanicus	Cocoons	India

Contd...

Table 2.6–Contd...

Species	*Commodity Damaged*	*Country*
Attagenus pellio	Cocoons	Germany, Georgia
Attagenus unicolor	Cocoons, Fabrics	USSR, North America
Attagenus unicolor japonicus	Cocoons, Raw silk, Floss, Fabrics	Japan
Trogoderma halsteadi	Cocoons	India
Trogoderma sternale	Cocoons, Raw silk	USA
Trogoderma varium	Cocoons, Eggs, Raw silk	Japan
Trogoderma versicolor	Cocoons, Raw silk	Georgia, Central Asia
Orphinus fulvipes	Cocoons	India
Anthrenus flavipes	Cocoons, Fabrics	Africa, India, Germany
Anthrenus museorum	Silk	Germany
Anthrenus pimpinellae	Cocoons	India
Anthrenus scrophularae	Silk	North America
Anthrenus verbasci	Cocoons, Raw silk, Fabrics, Eggs	Canada, Italy, Japan, USA
Trinodes rufescens	Cocoons, Raw silk	Japan

(b) Mites

Pediculoides ventricosus (Newport) commonly known as 'straw itch' mite belongs to the order Acarina and family Pediculoididae.

Seasonal Occurrence

Its occurrence has been reported throughout the country mostly from May to September.

Biology

The newly born mite is 0.2 mm in length and light yellow in colour. Males hatch earlier than females. Females are spindle shaped while males' oval shaped. Head is triangular. They have four pairs of legs with small claws. They are ovoviviparous. Females after mating and getting a suitable substratum attach themselves with claws and suckers. The young ones hatch out from the eggs in the female body and pass out in the form of adult like small acarid. Each adult female produces 100–150 young ones. There are 17 generations in a year and time taken to complete each generation is 7 to 18 days.

Symptoms and Nature of Damage

The acarid attacks larvae, pupae and adults of the silkworm. Acarid attaches itself to the soft skin of the host between the segments and obtains nutrition from there. They also produce a kind of toxin, which ultimately kills the host silkworm. After being infested, the larva stops feeding and become sluggish. The body of the host turns purple brown and silkworm starts vomiting yellowish brown fluid. The worms die within one or two days after infection.

Management

- ☆ On seeing the attack of acarid, rearing trays and appliances should be replaced.
- ☆ Disinfect the rearing appliances with steam.
- ☆ Wheat straw, rice straw or cotton should not be stored near the rearing house.

[3] Other Pests

(*a*) Birds

Birds are vertebrate warm-blooded animals and the total number of bird species known to science as inhabiting the earth today has been estimated to be about 8600. Birds cause considerable damage not only to growing field crops, fruit trees, orchards and threshing yards but also to sericultural crops.

Birds of Economic Importance Causing Damage to Crops

- ☆ House sparrow: *Passer domesticus*
- ☆ Parrot: *Psittacula eupatria; P. krameri; P. cyanocephala*
- ☆ Crow: *Corvus splendens*
- ☆ Pigeon: *Columba livia*
- ☆ Peacock: *Pava cristatus*
- ☆ Bulbul: *Pycnonotus cafer*
- ☆ Baya: *Ploceus philippinus*
- ☆ Myna: *Aeridothares tristis*
- ☆ Green bea eater: *Merops orientalis*
- ☆ Wild duck: *Pterocyanea discors*

House Sparrow

House sparrow belongs to class–Aves, order–Passeriformes, family–Passeridae, genus–*Passer*, species–*domesticus*. It is omnivorous, eats grains, insects, fruit buds, flower nectar and kitchen scraps. It causes severe damage to silkworm crops both under field conditions and in storage. It usually lives and builds its nest in a hole in ceiling niche in wall, inverted lampshade and every conceivable site within or without an occupied building.

Parrot

Parrot (*Psittacula eupatria; P. krameri; P. cyanocephala*) belongs to class–Aves, order–Psittaciformes, family–Psittacidae. It is one of the most familiar of Indian birds.

They often band into large flocks. It is highly destructive at all types to crops and fruits, gnawing and wasting far more that it actually eats and cause heavy damage to sericultural, agricultural and horticultural crops.

Crow

House crow belongs to class–Aves, order–Passeriformes, family–Corvidae, genus–*Corvus*, species–*splendens*. It is the most familiar bird of Indian towns and villages. Live in close association of man and obtain its livelihood from his works. They have been reported to cause heavy damage to maturing or ripe crops of sericultural, agricultural and horticultural importance. It is also a useful scavenger.

Management of Bird Pests

- ✰ *Destruction of Roosting Places*: This practice is applicable against parrot, myna (*Acridotheres tristis*) and other birds.
- ✰ *Trapping*: Some birds are trapped by using a sticky material. They are used for meat purpose.
- ✰ *Baiting*: Chapatti or grains soaked in insecticide solution can be used for killing some birds. Proper disposal of such birds is a necessity.
- ✰ *Destruction of Eggs*: Nests may be located and eggs destroyed.
- ✰ *Use of Bird Scarier*: Various devices like erecting a dummy model or making arrangement for beating of empty kerosene tins or acetylene guns to create loud noise at regular intervals.

(*b*) Rodents

Rodents belong to class–Mammalia, order–Rodentia, sub-order–Myomorpha, family–Muridae. They constitute the largest order of existing mammals. Management of rodents is a very intricate as well as a ticklish problem. Rodents infest an area throughout the year as compared to other pests which appear sporadically only for short period in certain seasons. Rodents continue to damage standing sericultural crops and stored cocoons. The following species of rats are important pests of sericultural crops in India.

Lesser Bandicoot or Field Rat (*Bandicota bengalensis*)

The field rat is dark grayish brown in colour with a grayish white belly and a bare tail; head and body 15–23 cm and tail 15–18 cm long. It makes large ramifying burrows in soil extending to a depth of 1–1.5 m and laterally 9–12m; the burrow along its course is provided with many walls or earthen blocks for protection. There are 4–5 openings for the burrow; the entrances are protected by heaps of excavated soil. Separate chambers for bed, breeding and food storage are provided in the burrow. It usually lives alone, one in a burrow. It feeds upon grass, grains and tubers and damage to many crops including sericultural crops. Once it starts damage in a particular area, it revisits the same area next night and spread the damage.

Grass Rat (*Millardia meltada*)

The grass rat is smaller in size, dark brownish gray above and pale gray below with soft fur. Head and body are about 13 cm long and tail 10 cm long. The burrows of the grass rat are similar to that of the field rat except that they are smaller in length and diameter and that usually more than one adult rat occupies a single burrow.

Indian Field Mouse (*Mus booduga*)

The body of the Indian field mouse is about 5–8 cm long with 5 cm long tail. It is brown in color with a white belly. It burrows in field bunds causing extensive damage to bunds and wastage of water.

Common Rat (*Rattus rattus*)

The common rat is reddish or yellowish brown with a pure white belly. It is destructive to tender parts of plants. It also damages stored silkworm cocoons. It lives and breeds inside nests specially constructed in the crowns of the plants. In closely planted gardens it can jump from plant to plant.

Gerbil Rat (*Tatera indica*)

The Indian gerbil rat is reddish grey in colour with white underside and it equals the common house rat in size with about 18 cm long head and body and hairy tail little longer than the head and body.

Common House Rat (*Rattus rattus rufescens*)

It is brownish grey with a dark undersurface and feed on all kinds of vegetable and animal food. It lives in roofs of houses and underground burrows. Its damage is great in warehouses and storage crops.

Integrated Rodent Management

The poisons used for the control of rodents are either acute poisons (single dose and quick acting) or chronic poison (multiple dose and slow acting). A rodenticide must have three ideal attributes–toxicity, acceptability and safety in use. The acute poisons are better for giving a quick knockdown, but they have little selectivity and poor efficacy. They require pre-baiting, as rodents develop bait shyness for them. Anticoagulants have advantage as far as efficacy and safety are concerned, but are slow in action, more labourious and hence the treatment cost is comparatively higher.

Rodenticides

(*i*) Zinc Phosphide

It is a grayish black powder having garlic odour of phosphine. Its toxicity is due to the release of phosphine gas from the molecule. Zinc phosphide baits are stable in air and non-acidic media, but when ingested, the acid present in stomach releases phosphine gas, which produces necrotic lesions and kidney damage causing death from heart failure. Death may occur within two hours of bait intake. It should not be used at a concentration above 2 per cent that may reduce the bait acceptability and increase poison aversion. Zinc phosphide is equally toxic to man, animals and poultry. Hence, dead rats should be removed from the vicinity immediately.

(*ii*) Anticoagulant Rodanticides

The first anticoagulant rodenticide compound developed was Warfarin. Bromadiolone was first registered in India and is in use since 1988. Anticoagulants constitute more than 95 per cent of total rodenticide usage.

- *Multi-dose Anticoagulants*: Warfarin and fumarin are used at 0.5 per cent concentration as fresh baits.
- *Single-dose Anticoagulants*: Bromadiolone used as single dose fresh bait (0.25 per cent), ready to use bait (0.005 per cent).

Plant Products

Certain plant products are known to cause anti-fertility effects *viz., Gloriosa supeprba, Cannabis sativa, Calotropis gigantia, Azadirachta indica* and can be used to control future generations.

Traps and Trapping

Live Traps

Pot trap, wonder trap and sherman trap are some of the live traps in use to trap rodents.

Kill Type Traps

Tanjore trap, arrow trap, bamboo trap, stone trap and break back (snap trap) are some of the kill type traps. Tanjore trap is used in the wetland fields. Break-back trap is used commonly in all places. Glue boards are newer type of trap where small boards (22 x 17.5 cm) are plastered with polybutanes and thickener for indoor use. Owl perches (50/ha) may be setup to reduce the menace of rats.

Chapter 3
Silkworm Diseases

The silkworm, *Bombyx mori* L., like any other insect, is prone to various diseases occurring in nature. Having been domesticated over centuries, it developed total dependence on man who has to take care of it. During its growth the silkworm comes in contact with various pathogens, and under the influence of the environment, the pathogen's capability to infect and its own capability to resist or succumb or co-exist, infection occurs. When the physiological equilibrium of the host is lost with the interference of the pathogen, a disease is said to occur. In general, outbreak of diseases during silkworm rearing and sometimes continuous crop failure has been usual phenomenon associated with tropical sericulture. The threat of the disease is associated with the factors like poor quality of mulberry leaf, unfavorable weather conditions, lack of independent rearing houses for effective disinfections, poor hygiene and above all faulty rearing practices. It is necessary to familiarize with the principles underlying the initiation, development and spread of silkworm diseases, to identify, prevent or cure to obtain a stable cocoon yield. In small and short-lived insects, it is difficult to treat and cure the disease besides which shall also be uneconomical. Prevention is therefore suggested in containing silkworm diseases.

Etiology of Silkworm Diseases

Each disease is caused by a specific pathogen known as an etiological agent. The causes include biological, chemical, nutritional, environmental and constitutional factors. The biological factors causing diseases are viruses, bacteria, fungi, protozoa and arthropods all of which are parasites; and all excepting arthropods are infectious. There is the phenomenon of cross-infection from one insect to the other.

Agro-chemicals, pyrethroids, exhaust gases from automobiles and factories, smoke, residue from disinfectants, etc. are among the chemical agents causing diseases. The chemical agents are non-parasitic and non-infectious. Physical agents include mechanical injury during rearing, feeding, spacing, mounting, sex separation of larvae/cocoons etc. Severe injury sometimes leads to instantaneous death, whereas mild injury weakens the larvae.

Silkworm diseases are broadly classified into two broad categories *viz.*, infectious and non-infectious diseases.

[A] Infectious Diseases

Infectious diseases are those caused by bacteria, virus, fungi, protozoa and similar microorganism, which enter and harm the body of the silkworm. The diseases can be transmitted from infected larvae to healthy larvae.

a) Viral Diseases

Nuclear polyhedrosis, Cytoplasmic polyhedrosis, Infectious flacherie and Densonucleosis.

b) Bacterial Diseases

Bacterial septicaemia, Bacterial toxicosis and Bacterial diseases of digestive tract.

c) Fungal Diseases

White Muscardine, Green Muscardine, Black Muscardine, Brown Muscardine and Aspergillosis.

d) Microsporidian Disease

Pebrine

[B] Non-infectious Diseases

Noninfectious diseases are those which are caused by arthropods, agricultural chemicals and mechanical injuries and that can not be transmitted from infected larvae to healthy larvae.

(*a*) *Arthropod*: Acarid infestation

(*b*) *Strings*: Euproctis similes, Setora postornata

(*c*) *Poisoning*: Agricultural chemicals, exhaust fumes, coal gas etc.

(*d*) *Physiological Ailments*

[A] Infectious Diseases

Major infectious diseases of silkworm prevailing in India and other countries are presented in Table 3.1.

Table 3.1: Status of Diseases of Mulberry Silkworm in India and Other Countries

Sl.No.	Disease	Pathogen	Prevalence in		Season
			India	Other Countries	
1.	**Viral**				
	Nuclear polyhedrosis	*Bm*NPV	Prevalent	Prevalent	Summer &
	Cytoplasmic polyhedrosis	*Bm*CPV	Rep. but not confirmed	-	rainy
	Infectious flacherie	*Bm*IFV	Prevalent	Prevalent	season
	Densonucleosis	*Bm*DNV1	Prevalent	Prevalent	
		*Bm*DNV2	Not Rep.	Not Rep.	
		*Bm*DNV3	Not Rep.	Not Rep	
2.	**Bacterial**				
	Bacterial diseases of digestive tract	*Streptococcus* sp., *Pseudomonas* sp	Prevalent	Prevalent	Summer & rainy season
	Bacterial septicaemia	*Bacillus* sp., *Serratia marcescens*	Prevalent	Prevalent	
	Bacterial toxicosis	*Bacillus thuringiensis*	Prevalent	Prevalent	
3.	**Fungal**				
	White muscardine	*Beauveria bassina*	Prevalent	Prevalent	Winter season
	Green muscardine	*Nomuraea rileyi*	Prevalent	Prevalent	

Contd...

Table 3.1–Contd...

Sl.No.	Disease	Pathogen	Prevalence in		Season
			India	Other Countries	
	Yellow muscardine	*Paecilomyces farinous*	Not reported	Prevalent	
	Red muscardine	*Sporosporelle uvella*	Not reported	Prevalent	
	Orange muscardine	*Sterigtnatocystis japonica*	Not reported	Prevalent	
	Aspergillosis	*Aspergillus flavus* *Aspergillus oryzae*	Prevalent	Prevalent	
4.	**Protozoan (Pebrine)**				
		Nosema bombycis	Prevalent	Prevalent	All seasons
		Nosema sp M -1 1	Prevalent	Prevalent	
		Nosema sp. M -1 4	Not reported	Prevalent	
		Vairomorpha sp M–12	Prevalent	Prevalent	
		Pleistophora sp. M–24	Not reported	Prevalent	
		Pleistophora sp. M–25	Not reported	Prevalent	
		Pleistophora sp. M–27	Not reported	Prevalent	
		Thelohania sp. M–32	Not reported	Prevalent	
		Leptomonas sp.	Not reported	Prevalent	

All diseases of silkworm *viz.*, protozoan, viral, bacterial and fungal are common in all rearing seasons. Concentrating on the prevention rather than trying to control them after their outbreak has largely overcome the problems of diseases. The improved rearing technology, package of practices for mulberry cultivation and preventive measures followed for diseases and pests of silkworm have improved the cocoon crop position. However, crop losses due to diseases in tropics continue to above 15–20 per cent.

[1] Viral Diseases

Virus is a biological entity, which lacks metabolism but undergoes multiplication at the expense of host cells. There are four kinds of silkworm diseases caused by viruses' *viz.*, Nuclear polyhedrosis, Cytoplasmic polyhedrosis, Infectious flacherie and Densonucleosis. Multiple infections are also common involving the pathogenesis by more than one pathogen in a host.

Viral diseases pose a serious threat to sericulture industry because these diseases occur in almost all seasons in general and the bad weather in particular. Inappropriate disinfection and poor management lead to serious outbreaks of the disease and inflicts significant severe losses to the cocoon crop. According to survey figures from some of the countries and areas, viral diseases account for almost 70-80 per cent of the total loss from silkworm diseases.

The viral diseases in silkworm are grouped into two categories:

(*a*) Inclusion/Occluded Type: Nuclear polyhedrosis and Cytoplasmic polyhedrosis.

(*b*) Non-inclusion/Non-occluded Type: Infectious flacherie, Gattine and Densonucleosis.

Inclusion type (nuclear and cytoplasmic polyhedrosis) can easily be identified through ordinary microscope while the non-inclusion type can be detected only through electron/fluorescent microscope and serological tests.

(*a*) Inclusion/Occluded Type

(*i*) Nuclear Polyhedrosis

Among the viral diseases, the nuclear polyhedrosis is most common and severe than other viral diseases in silkworm in India and several other countries. The disease occurs throughout the year but is more prevalent during summer and rainy seasons. The disease is also known as Grasserie, Milky disease, Fatty degeneration disease, Jaundice or Hanging disease.

Etiology

The etiological agent of this disease is the *Bombyx mori* Nuclear Polyhedrosis Virus (*Bm*NPV) belonging to the Sub-group 'A' of the family Baculoviridae, sub-family Eubaculovirinae which is a parasite principally on the nuclei of certain cells (trachea/epithelial cells, adipose tissue cells, dermal cells and blood cells).

The Virus

Paillot named the virus as *Borrelina bombycis*, which is rod shaped, with a size of 330 x 80 nm and consists of a membrane and a capsid, with the envelope being on the outside and the capsid at the center, and in between, the colloidal layer. Inside the capsid is the helical core. The capsid and the viral nucleic acid form the nucleo-capsid. Four layers of peplomer are found at the anterior part of the capsid, which may be the apparatus enabling absorption of the virus to take place. The nucleic acid is double stranded DNA (dsDNA). The viral particle contains 7.9 per cent nucleic acid, 77 per cent protein and also lipids and carbohydrates. The infective part of the virus is the nucleic acid, the protein part being non-pathogenic.

The Polyhedron

The polyhedra are visible under the 400 magnification of microscope, 2-6 microns in size, each being the shape of an octadecahedral hexahedron, sometime a trigon or a tetragon. Generally, in any one-cell nucleus, the sizes of the polyhedra are uniformly the same. The virus can exist both inside and outside the polyhedra. The former is called the polyhedra virus and the latter free virus. The stability of the polyhedral virus is greater than that of the free virus. The polyhedron is composed of 3–5 per cent viral particles, the rest being protein. It is highly refractile, with high density, insoluble in water and organic solvents but soluble in alkaline solutions. Thus, in the digestive tract of the silkworm the polyhedra dissolve, releasing the virions, which cause infection to the larvae. Virus inactivation occurs using bleaching powder solution containing 0.3 per cent active chlorine for three minutes, or 2 per cent formalin for 15 minutes.

Route of Infection and Pathogenesis

Infection by the virions and polyhedra is peroral. But, the free virus can also enter through the wounds. After being swallowed, the polyhedra on reaching the digestive tract are dissolved by the alkaline digestive fluids with the release of the virions. A portion of the virion is inactivated by the red fluorescent protein and excreted with the feces. Those particles, which escape inactivation, penetrate the peritrophic membrane, some enter the coelom and parasitize the susceptible cells there, and some may reside in the cells of the midgut, but the latter do not form polyhedra. *Bm*NPV forms polyhedra in the nuclei of tracheal cells, adipose tissue cells, dermal cells, blood cells and occasionally the nucleus of the middle and posterior portion of silk glands. The virus can multiply in the cell nucleus of the larval tissues and form polyhedra in it, the most susceptible cells being the hemolymph, tracheal epithelial cells, adipose tissue cells and dermal cells. The virions and the polyhedra progressively increase in number and size within the nucleus causing the nucleus to swell gradually. Bursting results from the accompanying distension of the whole cell. The free virus, polyhedra and cellular debris in the hemolymph of the infected larvae give the hemolymph its milky appearance. Parasitism of the dermal cells results in their dissolution, leaving only chitinous skin, which bursts easily.

Causes of the Disease

- ☆ Consuming contaminated leaf containing the pathogen.
- ☆ High temperature, high humidity and their sudden fluctuations.
- ☆ Excessive moisture in the rearing bed.
- ☆ Ineffective bed disinfection and insufficient ventilation.
- ☆ Feeding tender leaves during late instars.
- ☆ Overcrowding of larvae during rearing.
- ☆ Feeding inferior quality/unsuitable mulberry leaves.
- ☆ Use of surface contaminated laying.
- ☆ Larval starvation.

Alternate Host

*Bm*NPV is pathogenic to several lepidopteran insects including *Philosamia*, *Lymantria* and *Dendrolimus*. It is also known to infect *Samia ricini.*

Pathogen Persistence

The *Bm*NPV polyhedra have been recorded to persist in the rearing environment for 5 years as dry pills and 20 years at 4°C. The survival of virus suspended in haemolymph is better than in pure water. The occlusion bodies of baculovirus withstand freezing and thawing and can retain activity during prolonged exposure to normal temperature. The vaculoviruses persists for longer duration in soil. Various disinfectants *viz.*, formalin, sodium hypochlorite, lime, calcium hydroxide, chlorinated lime etc. are reported to be germicidal for *Bm*NPV.

Symptoms

- ☆ No external symptoms are noticed during early part of the disease except slightly sluggishness of the larvae.
- ☆ As the disease advances, appetite decreases and skin losses its tension. Initially, skin shows oily shining appearance, then it becomes thin and fragile and body becomes milky white with inter-segmental swellings.
- ☆ The diseased larvae in the final stage show pronounced swellings at the inter-segments resulting in bamboo cane like appearance of the larvae with distinct nodes.
- ☆ The fragile skin is prone to rupture easily, liberating liquefied body contents containing innumerable

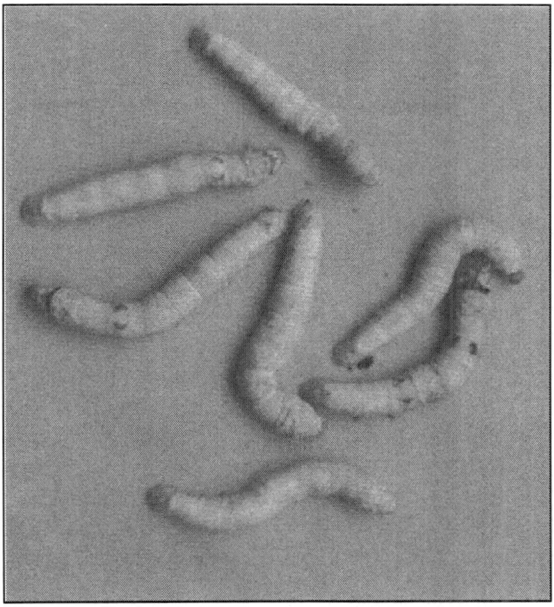

Grasserie Affected Silkworm Larvae (Early Stage)

Grasserie Affected Silkworm Larvae (Late Stage)

number of polyhedra, which become the source of contamination.

- ☆ If the disease occurs just before molting, larvae do not enter into molt.
- ☆ Infected larvae become restless and crawl aimlessly along the ridges or rims of rearing trays and subsequently falloff from the rearing tray on the ground, where they usually crawl in a circle and die.
- ☆ Death takes place after 4–5 days of infection in earlier stages and often 5–7 days in the later or grown up stages.
- ☆ Diseased larvae also lose clasping power of the pseudo and true legs except the caudal legs by which it clings with the head downward. Hence, the disease is also known as hanging disease.
- ☆ No external change is observed in pupae at the initial stages. However, towards the end skin is easily ruptured on handling as the poorly, infected worms fail to spin cocoons and die, whereby, if the infection is late, infected larvae are able to spin cocoons but die inside the cocoons.
- ☆ The cells of all infected tissues become abnormal.

Preventive Measures

- ☆ Silkworm rearing rooms, mulberry storage rooms, mounting rooms, equipments and rearing and grainage premises should be thoroughly disinfected.
- ☆ Surface disinfection of laying before brushing.

- ☆ Maintenance of proper temperature and humidity according to the requirement as per age and stage of development of larvae.
- ☆ Maintenance of proper hygienic conditions.
- ☆ Feeding nutritious mulberry leaves especially to young age silkworms.
- ☆ Provide constant fresh air circulation.
- ☆ Careful removal of diseased larvae and their proper disposal suitably by burning or by burying. The litter pit should be away from the rearing house.
- ☆ Change of infected seat paper and tray.
- ☆ Provide sufficient spacing according to the age and stage of larvae.
- ☆ Careful handling especially after moult.
- ☆ Keep bed thin and dry especially during rainy season.
- ☆ Application of bed disinfectant to prevent secondary contamination and spread of diseases *viz.*, Resham Keet Oushad (RKO), Vijetha, Labex, Resham Jyothi etc.

(*ii*) Cytoplasmic Polyhedrosis

It is one of the major diseases inflicting substantial economic loss to the sericulture industry. The disease occurs mainly during summer season. Over 221 known insect species are susceptible to Cytoplasmic Polyhedrosis Viruses (CPVs). Of these 80 per cent are Lepidoptera, 16 per cent Diptera, 3 per cent Hymenoptera and less than 1 per cent are Coleopteran and Neuropteran (Hukuhara, 1991).

Etiology

The virus causing cytoplasmic polyhedrosis is the *Bombyx mori* Cytoplasmic Polyhedrosis Virus (*Bm*CPV) belonging to the cytoplasmic polyhedral group of the family Reoviridae and genus Cypovirus that multiplies in the midgut and columnar cells. CPV of insects are the only group of family Reoviridae characterized by presence of polyhedral inclusion bodies, located in cytoplasm of virus-infected cells in the mid-gut epithelium. The inclusion bodies are hexagonal or tetragonal.

The Virus

The virus particle is globular, 60–70 nm in size, icosahedra hexahedron; each capsomere extends outward to a four-jointed projection the tip of which carries a globular body concealing the two distal joints. The capsid consists of two icosahedral coats, which are linked together by a tubular structure at the apposing apices. At the center of the capsid lies the core. The nucleic acid is of the double stranded type and is RNA.

The Polyhedron

The cytoplasmic polyhedral virus (CPV) parasitizes mainly the cytoplasm of the midgut cylindrical cells where polyhedra are formed. The polyhedron is an icosahedral hexahedron, sometimes a tetragon or a trigon. The polyhedra inside the same cell do not show uniform size, with great variation 1–10 microns approximately. The physical and chemical properties of the polyhedra are similar to those of NPV, but resistance to formalin is greater, requiring 5 hours treatment before the virus is inactivated. Thus, if formalin is selected for rearing room disinfection, 0.5 per cent freshly prepared lime must be added to make the disinfectant solution in order to enhance the efficacy of disinfection.

Route of Infection and Pathogenesis

Infection is mainly peroral. The virus and polyhedra enter the digestive tract with mulberry leaves swallowed. The process of invasion of the mid-gut cells is still not well understood. Using uridine tracer it has been demonstrated that RNA is first synthesized inside the nucleus then transferred to the cytoplasm. The formation of polyhedral proteins also takes place in the cytoplasm, after which the virions are enclosed to form polyhedra. *Bm*CPV forms polyhedra first in the cytoplasm of mid-gut epithelial cell and then in the goblet cells and regenerative cells.

The digestive and absorptive capacities of the mid-gut are impaired, which together with expenditure of large quantities of host protein to form viral polyhedral proteins cause disturbances in nucleic acid and protein metabolism. As a result the free amino-acid pool of the tissues decreases. All this leads to physiological dysfunction and disease.

Causes of the Disease

- ☆ Presence of pathogen in contaminated diet/ mulberry leaf.
- ☆ Inferior quality of mulberry leaves.
- ☆ Physiological disturbance of larva under high temperature and humidity and their fluctuation.
- ☆ Improper ventilation and accumulation of poisonous gas.
- ☆ Use of improperly decomposed silkworm litter to the mulberry garden.
- ☆ Accumulation of faecal matter in the bed.

Pathogen Stability

The *Bm*CPV is stable and persists for a period of about one year under laboratory conditions and 15-30 days in soil. Exposure of pathogen to sunlight for 6-7 hr, temperature of 100°C for 5 sec., 90°C for 10 sec. and 70°C for 30 min and 60°C for 20 hr also inactivate the virus. Chemicals such as formalin 5 per cent, slaked lime at 0.5 per cent, chlorinated lime at 0.5 per cent, calcium hydroxide at 0.5 per cent and pH of 3.8 kills the pathogen. The environmental temperature influences the infection and multiplication of pathogen.

Alternate Host

The *Bm*CPV has been observed to inflict *Philosamia, Theophilia and Dendrolimus* etc. The CPV from *S. littura, Lymantria* and *Theophilia* are found to infect *Bombyx mori*.

Symptoms

- ☆ Larvae show symptoms of sluggishness, loose appetite, cease feeding and sometimes develops diarrhoea and vomit gut juice.
- ☆ Larvae lag behind in their growth and development.
- ☆ Head becomes disproportionately large and translucent and body shrunken.
- ☆ Frequent expulsion of semi solid and whitish faecal matter.
- ☆ If observed through the dorsal integument, the mid-gut looks pale white.
- ☆ In severely infected larvae, mid-gut becomes chalky white and opaque. The whitening starts from posterior portion of the mid-gut and slowly progress towards the anterior portion.

Cytoplasmic Polyhedrosis Virus Affected Larvae

- ☆ Anal region is soiled and occasionally rectal protrusion is noticed.
- ☆ On dissection of infected larvae, mid-gut is seen as whitish and opaque compared to greenish and transparent mid-gut of healthy larvae.
- ☆ Infected pupae are generally smaller than normal and the infected moth lays fewer eggs and is short lived.

Preventive Measures

- Effective disinfection of rearing room and appliances.
- Proper incubation of silkworm eggs.
- Young silkworm should be reared in co-operative chawki rearing centers with climatic control and hygienic conditions under the guidance of capable expert.
- Young larvae should be fed with good quality mulberry leaves harvested from garden exclusively meant for young stages.
- Avoid growing mulberry in phosphorus deficient soil, under shade and high alkaline and acidic soil condition.
- Provide sufficient ventilation especially during 5th instars.
- Provide optimum temperature and humidity required for different ages of larvae.
- Provide required spacing according to the age and stage of larvae.
- Care in disposal of litter as cytoplasmic polyhedrosis contaminates through faecal matter.
- Destroy the diseased larvae; faecal matter and bed refuse either by burning or by decomposition in a manure pit.
- Breeding of resistant strains of silkworm.
- Chemicals like 1 per cent calcium hydroxide can be sprayed on mulberry leaf and fed to larvae to reduce the occurrence of the disease.

(*b*) Non Inclusion/Non-Occluded Type

(*i*) Infectious Flacherie

Infectious flacherie is highly contagious viral flacherie in silkworm caused by Picornavirus (Pico = very small) of family Picarnaviridae. It is a 'sub-chronic' disease resulting primarily due to the physiological disorders and secondarily by the infection of bacterium. The term flacherie is a general one used to include dysentery conditions due to microbial and amicrobial factors in silkworm. Flacherie may be due to virus, bacteria and physiological disorders. Infectious flacherie is found in the entire silkworm rearing areas of the world. It is highly contagious and exceedingly disastrous condition occurring mainly in the summer and autumn rearing season.

Etiology

This disease is caused by the *Bombyx mori* Infectious Flacherie Virus (*Bm*IFV) belonging to the family Picornaviridae. The Picornaviruses are among the smallest viruses in the animal kingdom.

The Virus

The virus particle is globular, about the size of 30 nm; the ultra structure is still undetermined; the nucleic acid is single stranded RNA and no polyhedra are formed. The virus exhibits high virulence, and in the body of the dead larvae it may retain its pathogenicity even after 2–3 years in the rearing room. The virus in the feces can withstand 100°C for 30 minutes without being destroyed, but treatment with 2 per cent formalin or bleaching powder containing 0.3 per cent active chlorine or 0.5 per cent lime paste for 3 minutes can achieve inactivation.

Route of Infection and Pathogenesis

Infection mainly takes place per orally. After the virus enters the digestive tract the red fluorescent protein inactivates a portion of the virus. Auto radiographic techniques show that *Bm*IFV infects the goblet cells of the mid-gut by their ssRNA. The latter further gains entrance into the nucleus where it replicates to form new ssRNA. Later on, the newly formed ssRNA is transferred to the cytoplasm and together with the viral protein is assembled into viral particles. Infection starts from the anterior region of the mid-gut and then progress towards posterior region.

The IFV chiefly infects the goblet cells of the mid-gut which perform the function of secreting digestive fluids and which in turn are not only having the capacity to digest the mulberry leaves but also have bacteriostatic properties. Degeneration of the goblet cells affects the digestive and bacteriostatic functions, and this permits rapid proliferation of bacteria. Under the concerted invasion of virus and bacteria, mortality of the silkworm is accelerated.

Pathogen Stability

The environmental factors influence the pathogen stability. The viral activity is reduced at pH 2 and active between 3 -12. The pH for optimum activity is 6.0. Formalin of 0.25 per cent concentration inactivates the virus in 30 min and sunlight in 6–7 hr. Slaked lime in 30 min, 0.3 per cent chlorine in 3 min, HCl 15 per cent at 48°C in 6 min kill the virus.

Alternate Host

Infectious flacherie virus has been observed to inflict *Bombyx mandarina*. The pathogen multiplies in the mid-gut epithelium cells but the larvae remain healthy. *Glyphodes pyloalis*, a common pest of mulberry is also a habitual alternate host for *Bm*IFV as well as *Bm*DNV.

Causes of the Disease

- ✰ Virus is liberated freely along with faecal matter and contaminates leaves in trays.
- ✰ Virus exists freely in air, water, mulberry leaves and dead larvae.

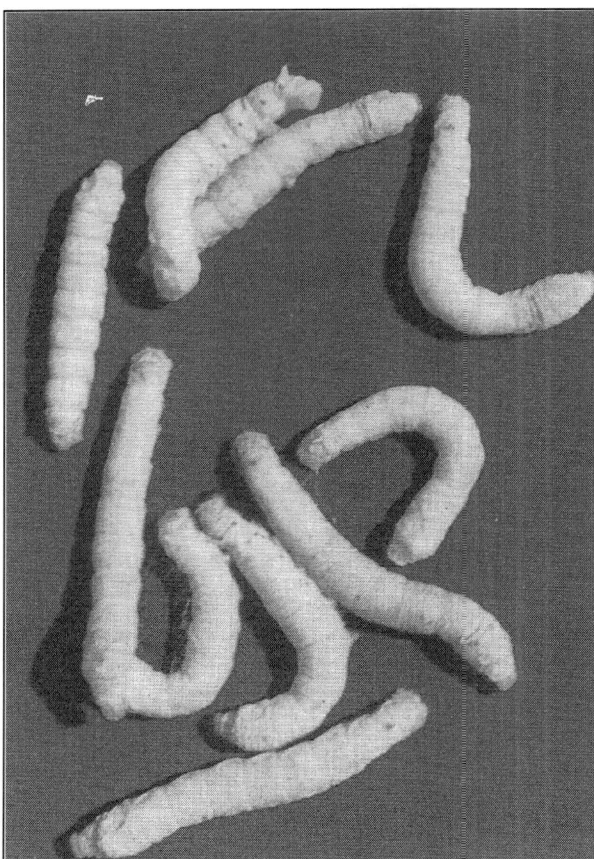

Infectious Flacherie Virus Affected Larvae

Symptoms

- ☆ Similar to bacterial flacherie.
- ☆ Loss of appetite and translucent cephalothorax.
- ☆ Look sluggish and sick with head and thorax motionless.
- ☆ Larvae with disproportionately enlarged head compared to healthy worms.
- ☆ Retarded growth and development followed by shrinkage of the body.
- ☆ Infected larvae evacuate excreta in chain or string or irregular shaped.
- ☆ Diarrhoea followed by vomiting gastric juice.
- ☆ The body turns transparent and the gut is filled with brownish fluid.
- ☆ Some individuals may exhibit rectal protrusion.
- ☆ Diagnosis by external symptom is difficult and the disease can be detected by fluorescent antibody technique or by staining the infected cells with pyronine methyl green.
- ☆ Latex agglutination and other serological tests are also being used for the detection of the disease.

Preventive Measures

- ☆ Select races resistant to infectious flacherie.
- ☆ Young silkworms are reared in co-operative units under strict hygienic condition.
- ☆ The diseased larvae should be picked up and destroyed.
- ☆ Feed with nutritious mulberry leaves to keep sound health. Too mature leaves at early instars and tender leaves at later instars should be avoided.

- ☆ Soiled and diseased leaves moist with raindrops should also be avoided for feeding.
- ☆ As the virus exhibits high virulence and may retain its pathogenecity in the body of dead larvae for 2–3 years, the rearing rooms, appliances and rearing surroundings must be thoroughly disinfected with effective disinfectant *i.e* by using 2 per cent formalin and 0.5 per cent calcium hydroxide or bleaching powder containing 1 per cent active chlorine.
- ☆ Provide favorable environmental conditions during rearing.
- ☆ The diseased larvae with bed refuse should be burnt or put in manure pit for thorough decomposing.
- ☆ The faecal and litter of diseased larvae are piled in a manure pit for decomposition.

(*ii*) Densonucleosis Disease

Densonucleosis viruses of viral family Parvoviridae cause the disease. The entomopathogenic members of the family occur in the genus Densovirus and are called Densonucleosis virus (DNV). DNV was first isolated from the larvae of greater wax moth, *Galleria mellonella* (*Gm*DNV) and later similar viruses were isolated from orders Lepidoptera, Diptera, Orthoptera, Odonata etc. Densonucleosis in silkworm prevails throughout the year in all sericultural countries. There are reports of its occurrence and causing extensive damage in China and India. The host insect species infected with DNV are distributed all over the world as listed in Table 3.2.

Table 3.2: Host Insect Species Infected with DNV

Host	*Country of Isolation*	*Year of Isolation*
Lepidoptera		
Agalis uricae	United Kingdom	1973
Agraulic vanillae	United Kingdom	1980
Bombyx mori	Japan and China	1973 and 1982
Euxoa auxillaris	United States	1970
Galleria mellonella	France	1964
Pieries rapae	China	1977
Sibine fuscae	France	1977
Diptera		
Aedes egyptii	Soviet Union	1972
Simulin vittatum	United States	1976
Odonata		
Lencorrhina dubia	Sweden	1979
Orthoptera		
Periplaneta fulginosa	Japan	1979

Source: Kawase and Kurstak, 1990.

Causative Agent

In silkworm, non-occluded virus belonging to the genus Densovirus of the family Parvoviridae causes the disease in *Bombyx mori*. The virus *Bm*DNVs attack the nuclei of mid gut columnar cells. The *Bombyx mori* DNVs are categorized into three groups, *viz*., *Bm*DNV1, *Bm*DNV2 and *Bm*DNV3. The size of *Bm*DNV1, *Bm*DNV2 and *Bm*DNV3 are approximately 22 ± 0.5 nm, 21–23 nm and 23–24 nm respectively. The serological studies with the antiserum against purified *Bm*DNV revealed that the virus is serologically different from IFV of silkworm as well as DNV isolated from *Galleria mellonella* (Watanabe, 1981).

Route of Infection

Infection usually takes place through per oral or by induction. The major source of contamination is the virus excreted along with the faeces by the silkworm. The pathogen persists for over one month in rearing house conditions and 30–60 days in the soil. However, the virus is inactivated when exposed for 10 hr to direct sunlight under dry conditions or 20 hr in humid conditions. The virus loses its activity at 80°C for 5 minutes. It is estimated that during the larval period of 24–26 days, the pathogen multiply in 8–13 cycles.

Alternate Host

Mulberry pyralid, *Glyphodes pyloalis* is an important alternate source of pathogen.

Symptoms

- ☆ Retarded growth, loss of appetite, shrinkage of body and lack of body flaccidity.
- ☆ Translucent cephalothoracic region.
- ☆ Dissected alimentary canal of the larvae appears pale yellow in color without most of the content.
- ☆ Head and thorax upheld motionless.
- ☆ Irregular shaped faeces with high moisture content.
- ☆ Gut filled with brownish fluid.
- ☆ Per orally infected larvae usually die after seven days.

Control and Preventive Measures

- ☆ Control pyrallid moth in the mulberry field, which is a major contaminative agent.

Densonucleosis Virus Affected Silkworm Larvae

- ✰ Stop cross infection through silkworm faeces and rearing bed.
- ✰ Early detection and rejection of batches found to be infected with virus through fluorescent antibody study.
- ✰ Rear non-susceptible breeds or crosses.
- ✰ Rear silkworms under congenial conditions of environment and nutrition.
- ✰ Spray of 0.3 per cent slaked lime solution in addition to usual disinfection procedure is recommended in case of high incidence of disease in the previous crop.

Staining Procedure for Polyhedra of NPV and CPV

For identification of polyhedra of NPV and CPV following procedure is adopted:

- ☆ Make a smear of polyhedra on a slide and air dry.
- ☆ Fix in methyl alcohol for 5 sec and air dry.
- ☆ Stain in Giemsa for 45–60 minutes (1 or 2 drops of stock giemsa stain to 1 ml of distilled water).
- ☆ Wash in distilled water.
- ☆ Air dry or blot dry and mount in DPX.
- ☆ Examine under high power of microscope.
- ☆ Polyhedra stained in violet blue.

(*iii*) Gattine Disease

Causative Agent

It is a complex disease caused by combination of two pathogens. An ultra non-inclusion type of virus affects the cylindrical epithelial cells causing nuclear lesions and a bacterium *Streptococcus bombycis* is a secondary invader to complete the symptoms. It is popularly known as Salpa (Bengal) and Hasirumoto (Karnataka) disease. *Streptococcus bombycis* plays a significant role in the development of gattine, although it is not the principal cause. The virus excreted along with faeces causes contamination during rearing. A submicroscopic virus causes the gattine but it alone does not significantly alter the pH of the intestinal contents of the diseased larvae from that of healthy silkworm. Due to invasion of *Streptococci* the intestinal contents characteristically become more alkaline. The symptoms of gattine manifested, only when the combination of *Streptococcus* and virus occurs in the susceptible silkworm.

Symptoms

- ☆ The cephalic portion is swollen and almost transparent.

- ☆ The thorax and interior part of gut are devoid of mulberry leaf, but fully occupied with gastric juice.
- ☆ Lack of appetite and ejection of clearly ropy liquid from mouth, which is slightly alkaline than the normal secretion.

Control and Preventive Measures

- ☆ Maintenance of strict hygienic condition and congenial environmental conditions.
- ☆ Larvae infected should be immediately removed and destroyed.
- ☆ Thorough disinfection of rearing rooms and equipments.

[2] Bacterial Diseases

Bacterial diseases affecting silkworms are collectively known as 'Flacherie' or 'Kalashira'. Its occurrence is associated with environmental factors like temperature and relative humidity and unevenness in these factors creates physiological and metabolic abnormalities in silkworm larvae. The incidence of flacharie is high during hot and humid seasons. However, the massive outbreak of this disease is not common but depending upon the poor disinfections, accumulation of contaminated mulberry leaves, improper handling and unsafe use of bacterial pesticides, sometimes causes large-scale loss in crops. Other attributed causes are high temperature, high humidity, bad ventilation, bad quality leaves (dirty leaf, coarse leaf, leaf not suited to the age and stage of the larvae, wet and fermented leaf etc.), over feeding, decreased alkalinity.

Infection takes place due to some disturbances in the metabolic activity of the caterpillar. When the alkalinity of the gut is reduced, the bacteria, which are normally present on the mulberry leaves, find a medium in which they multiply rapidly. Matsura renowned scientist reported that worms fed on leaves containing little chlorophyll also suffer from flacharie. Improper feeding also renders silkworms susceptible to the diseases. Infected worms becomes soft, skin elasticity is lost and vomit yellowish fluid. Initially larvae become yellowish in color, then turn brown and finally become dark black after death. That is why, the disease is also known as Kalashira. Due to bacterial purification, internal organs of diseased larvae become liquidified ailing all sorts of dysenteries. In general vomiting, diarrhoea, thickening of peritrophic membrane, brown/yellowish color of gut contents, discoloration of body and purification accompanied by blackening of body is the symptoms of larvae suffering from flacharie.

Flacharie disease of silkworms is caused not by any special bacterium but by sets of bacteria, which occur on mulberry leaves. The important ones are *Streptococcus pastorlanus, Streptococcus bombycis, Bacillus megatehum, Bacillus sotto, Bacillus A, Bacillus coli, Bacillus mycoides, Micrococcus etc.* Bacterial diseases of silkworms are divided into three major types:

(*i*) Bacterial diseases of digestive organs

(*ii*) Bacterial septicemia

(*iii*) Sotto or bacterial toxicosis.

(*i*) Bacterial Diseases of Digestive Organs

Causative Agent

The disease is also known as 'Transparent Head Disease'. Various theories have been advocated as the cause of this disease. These are–the bacterial theory, the non-bacterial theory and the intermediate theory. The intermediate theory has been widely accepted. Multiplication of bacteria in digestive tract leads to the swelling and transparency of head. The bacteria associated with the progress of disease are gram-positive *Streptococcus* sp. belonging to the family Streptocceae. Under poor nourishment and adverse environmental and rearing conditions, the physiological metabolic activity of the digestive tract is disturbed which is responsible for the disease. There is no doubt that poor quality of mulberry leaves provided to the larvae particularly during the chawki rearing is one of the major reason for the outbreak of the disease during the final stage of fifth instars larvae. For example if weather remains cloudy or rainy for a long time or temperature is much higher than the desired level or if just before brushing unhealthy conditions prevail, the quality of mulberry leaves deteriorate fast and if these leaves are supplied to the silkworms for feeding during 1st to 3rd instars, the larvae become victim of the disease during 5th instars.

Route of Infection

Per-oral

Predisposing Factors

- ✰ High temperature and high humidity and their fluctuation.

- ☆ Poor nourishment.
- ☆ Inadequate ventilation especially in fifth instar.
- ☆ Overcrowding and starvation of larvae.
- ☆ Decreased alkalinity of gut.
- ☆ Feeding insecticide poisoned mulberry leaf.

Symptoms

- ☆ Poor appetite, sluggish movement and translucent cephalothoracic and head region.
- ☆ Stunted body size and retarded body growth.
- ☆ Oral and anal discharges.
- ☆ Affected worms hide under the mulberry leaves.
- ☆ Worms affected in the late stage remain for a long period without spinning cocoons.
- ☆ In majority of cases body becomes black but some times it turns red due to presence of *Bacillus prodigiosis* or green because of presence of *Bacillus pyocyaneus*.

Preventive Measures

- ☆ Proper incubation of surface disinfected layings.
- ☆ Selection of race resistant to unfavorable conditions.
- ☆ Feed nutritious quality mulberry leaves and regulate feeds according to the age and stage of silkworms as recommended.
- ☆ Maintain optimum temperature, humidity and proper environmental and hygienic conditions.
- ☆ Provide sufficient ventilation.
- ☆ Avoid overcrowding of larvae in the rearing bed.

- ☆ Add chloramphenicol (0.05 per cent) to the diet.
- ☆ Remove diseased larvae from the rearing bed as soon as it is observed.
- ☆ Avoid cold storage of freshly hatched larvae.
- ☆ Ensure careful handling of silkworm larvae during molting phase.

(*ii*) Bacterial Septicemia

Bacteria reside and multiply enormously in haemolymph of larvae, pupae and moths. Septicemia during larval stages leads to larval mortality, whereas, infection during pupal stage leads to a large number of melted cocoons, thus affecting egg production on one hand and making it unsuitable for reeling on the other.

Causative Agent

Streptococci, Staphylococci and *Bacilli*

Route of Infection

Usually through wounds or injury of skin, rarely peroral.

Septicemia is of two types:

Black Thorax Septicemia

It is caused by gram-positive *Bacillus* species belonging to the family Bacillaceae of the order Eubacteriales. These are gram positive, spore-forming rod shaped bodies occurring either singly or in chains. It takes just 10 hrs to kill the larvae at 28°C. At higher temperature and under epidemic conditions, the infected larvae will die within 5–6 hrs. The size of *Bacillus* is 1–1.5 x 3 microns, spores sub-terminal and flagella peritrichate.

Black Thorax Septicemia Affected Silkworm Larvae

Red Septicemia

It is caused by gram-negative *Serratia marcescens*. The disease is also known as 'Court' in Europe and 'Rangi' in India. They are gram negative and non-sporulating. It is minor bacterial disease. *Serratia marcescens* occurred singly or in small chains causes it. They are non-sporulating. The genus *Serratia* usually produces a characteristic red or pink pigment, although sometimes white or rose strain also occurs. They are 0.6–1.0 x 0.5 microns in size and look like small rods, flagella peritrichate with rose red colonies.

Differences Between Black and Red Septicemia

In black septicemia blackening starts from thorax and extends to the dorsal vessel till the whole body darkens and rots. In red septicemia whole body softens taking a slightly reddish tinge. The disease is identified by the crimson red color of the affected silkworm larvae and pupae at the time of death or after death.

Symptoms

- Pro-legs lose their clasping power.
- Loss of appetite and lethargic nature.
- Body shrinks, thoracic region swollen and larvae vomit fluid.
- Excretion of soft and liquid like excrements.
- Affected larvae after death exhibit brown, green or intermediate colour.
- Fore intestine swollen and the posterior part shrunken in dead larvae.
- Rupturing body wall emit foul smell.

Pathogenesis

The bacteria exist mainly in the natural environment, in the soil and adhering to the dust particles, sewage and on mulberry leaves, in the rearing rooms and appliances. Warm and humid environment (high temperature and humidity) is most favorable for the propagation of these bacteria. These diseases occur mostly at the later part of the larval life. They mostly infect silkworms through wounds and multiply rapidly in the haemolymph.

Preventive Measures

High temperature and high humidity conditions are

most favorable for the propagation of the bacteria responsible for the disease. Therefore, this disease occurs in the seasons having high temperature and humidity. Irrespective of the health of the larvae, the disease is transmitted mainly through injury or wound and multiplies in haemolymph disrupting the normal physiological functions causing septicemia. Major preventive measures are:

- ✰ Avoid injury or wounds to silkworms and pupae.
- ✰ General disinfection.
- ✰ Isolate and destroy diseased larvae by burning or burying deep in the soil.
- ✰ Maintain hygienic conditions.
- ✰ Avoid overcrowding.
- ✰ Avoid accumulation of faeces in rearing beds.

(*iii*) Bacterial Toxicosis/Sotto Disease

Causative Agent

Toxicosis in silkworm is caused by different strains of *Bacillus thuringiensis*. It belongs to the order–Eubacteriales and family–Bacilliaceae. The member of the family consists of undifferentiated rigid cells, which are either spherical or straight rods. It produces a toxic substance and the disease is toxicosis. The toxin produced is dissolved in the alkaline gut juice, absorbed through the gut wall, affecting the nervous system, causing spasm and paralysis. In Bt strain, 7 different toxin have been reported:

- ✰ Phosphalipase (BT- exotoxin)
- ✰ Thermostable exotoxin (BT B-exotoxin)
- ✰ Enzyme–may not be toxin (BT Y-exotoxin)

- ☆ Protein parasporal crystal (BT- endotoxin)
- ☆ Labile toxin
- ☆ Water soluble toxin isolated from commercial formulate
- ☆ A mouse factor exotoxin

Chronic Bacterial Toxicosis

It is caused by ingestion of small quantity of Bt crystal toxin. Mulberry leaf intake is reduced, faeces become irregular shaped and occasional vomiting occurs. Thorax and abdominal tips become transparent and muscles develop paralysis. The other symptoms of infected larvae are loss of clasping power of the legs, softness of skin, retarded growth and light brown coloration.

Acute Bacterial Toxicosis

The symptoms are lack of appetite, sluggishness, lack of skin tension followed by shrinkage of body, diarrhoea, constipation, loss of clasping power of legs, lifting of head, paralysis followed by death. The death may occur within 10 minutes to a few hours. The body of insect becomes black shortly after death. The time from initial infection to death is shorter when temperature and humidity are higher. The corpse becomes dark brown and the inner organs of body are liquidified. If the skin bursts, a black foul smelling liquid oozes out.

Route of Infection

Per-oral

Symptoms

- ☆ Lack of appetite, skin tension, sluggishness followed by shrinkage of the body.

Sotto Disease Affected Silkworm Larvae

- Diarrhoea and loss of clasping power of legs.
- Spasm and paralysis and even body twisting.
- Vomiting yellow fluid.
- After death body becomes black with internal organs liquefied.
- After death the head appears hook shaped.
- Skin is fragile, easily cracks and liberates foul smelling liquid.

Preventive Measures

- Thorough disinfection of rearing rooms and appliances.

- Disease spread through faecal matter and hence removes diseased larvae and destroys them.
- Larvae must be prevented for swelling of toxic substances.
- Various strains of *B. thuringiensis*, which are using as biological insecticides should be assessed for their toxicity against silkworm and strains toxic to silkworm should not used in silkworm growing areas.
- Treatment with 0.05 per cent and 1 per cent Sodium hypochlorite for 1–30 minutes reduced both the viability and infectivity.
- Streptomycin sulphate, Gentacixcin, Cloxocillin and Kanamycin at 0.05 per cent and 1 per cent concentration supplemented through mulberry leaf as feed to silkworm leads to lowering the occurrence of the disease.

Techniques for Bacterial Staining

Crystal-violet Saffranin Method

- Make a bacterial smear on a slide and heat it by passing the slide on the flame.
- Immerse the slide in ammonium oxalate crystal violet stain for one minute.
- Rinse the slide in running tap water for 5 seconds.
- Rinse quickly with 'Gram iodine' solution and immerse in it for one minute.
- Dip the slide in 'n-propyl alcohol' for one minute and give three changes separately for one minute in each.

- ☆ Counter stain in saffranin for one minute.
- ☆ Mount in DPX and observe under oil immersion.
- ☆ Gram-positive bacteria take blue stain and gram-negative red stain.

Preparation of Solution

(a) Ammonium Oxalate Crystal Violet Solution

Solution A: Dissolve 2 gm of crystal violet in 40 ml of 95 per cent ethyl alcohol.

Solution B: Dissolve 1.6 gm of ammonium oxalate in 160 ml of distilled water. Mix solutions A and B.

(b) Grams' Iodine Solution

First dissolve 2 gm of potassium iodide in 5 ml of distilled water and add 1 gm of iodine. To this solution add 295 ml of distilled water.

Immune Responses to Bacterial Infection

Immunity is a type of resistance to disease in which an organism is resisting a pathogen and thus resisting the development of the disease. Immunity is an added ability acquired naturally and or artificially. Immunity can be divided into two categories:

(*a*) Naturally acquired (Active and passive)

(*b*) Artificially acquired (Active and passive)

Immunity is the result of the role played by numerous factors largely mechanical and physiological in nature. An immunity that has been gained by an organism during its lifetime is known as acquired immunity. Naturally an infectious agent acquires acquired immunity as a result of an attack and artificially acquired immunity is due to infectious agents or vaccines inoculated into the insect. All of these in turn may be active or passive. Active immunity is one in which the host has a direct or active participation. Along with the production of antibodies by the host itself, there is usually an accompanying increased cellular reactivity and a general increase in resistance to the microorganism concerned. Passive immunity occurs to a host that is the recipient of antibodies formed in the body of animal of the same or different species. It involves no active generation of protective substances by the immunized insect.

Thatte Disease

Relatively recently, a new silkworm disease has been reported in some parts of Karnataka. Farmers called it Thatte (meaning tray) disease. The disease is noticed in the rainfed areas of Mysore and Chamrajnagar districts.

Symptoms

- ☆ Sudden death of silkworms at 4th and 5th day of 5th instar and sometimes in 4th instar.
- ☆ The larvae die patch by patch in rearing trays.
- ☆ Thatte disease larvae look normal without showing unequal or any other morphological symptoms and start dying.
- ☆ The worms die within 10 hrs from the appearance of 1st symptom of the disease.
- ☆ The dead larvae show more of flacherie symptoms like flaccid body, blackening of skin, vomiting and diarrhoea prior to death.

Preventive Measures

- ✰ Cross ventilation especially during 5th instar should be ensured.
- ✰ The rearing houses should be thoroughly disinfected 2-3 times using 5 per cent bleaching powder.
- ✰ Bed disinfection after each moult.
- ✰ Use of cow dung to smear the tray should be discouraged.

[3] Fungal Diseases

Fungal diseases (mycosis) in silkworm are caused by parasitic fungi. Two major kinds of such diseases are Muscardine and Aspergillosis. There are more than 10 types of fungi, which cause Muscardine, and signs of the disease vary with the type of infecting fungus. Depending on the color of the spores of fungus, which covers the body of the silkworm giving characteristic color have been named as white muscardine, green muscardine, yellow muscardine, black muscardine, red muscardine etc. The different types of muscardine and their causal organism are presented in Table 3.3.

Depending on the color of dead larvae and the causative agent, they are divided into white muscardine, green muscardine, yellow muscardine, red muscardine, purplish red muscardine and black muscardine.

(*i*) White Muscardine

Causative Agent

Beauveria bassiana belonging to the family Moniliceae, order Moniliales of the class Fungi Imperfecti. White muscardine in silkworm is commonly known as Sunna katu roga. The disease is prevalent in all sericultural countries.

Table 3.3: Different Kinds of Muscardines Infecting Silkworm

Muscardine Type	*Causal Organism*
White muscardine	*Beauveria bassiana*
Green muscardine	*Spicaria prasina*
Yellow muscardine	*Paecilomyces farinosus*
Black muscardine	*Beauveria brongniartti, Metarrhizium anisopliae*
Red muscardine	*Sporosporella uvella*
Yellow red muscardine	*Paecilomyces fumosorosea*
Purplish-red muscardine	*Spicaria rubida*
Orange muscardine	*Sterigmatocystis japonica*
Aspergillosis/ Brown muscardine	*Aspergillus flavus/ Aspergillus tamari*
Pencillosis	*Penicillum citrinum P. granulatum*

Route of Infection

Through body contamination *i.e*, direct penetration of the skin by germinating conidia. Main sources of contaminations are mummified larvae, infected seat paper, tray and dead wild lepidopterous larvae from the mulberry field. The disease is highly contagious as the conidia are air borne. This disease occurs during rainy and winter seasons under low temperature and high humidity. The developmental cycle of Beauveria consists of conidium, vegetative mycelium and aerial mycelium. The conidium is colorless, globular or oval in shape. Under favorable conditions of temperature and humidity, the conidium germinates within 8-10 hours of coming in contact with the body of the silkworm. On germination, it penetrates the body wall for further multiplication. After some time, the vegetative hyphae come out of the skin to form aerial hyphae bearing innumerable conidiophores. These conidiophores give rise to small branches, which bear one or two conidia.

Symptoms

- ☆ Loss of appetite, inactiveness and lethargic condition.
- ☆ Loss of skin elasticity.
- ☆ Diarrhoea followed by vomiting and death.
- ☆ Initially, soon after death body of dead larvae is elastic and smooth.
- ☆ 0–10 hrs after death, it hardens (crystals of ammonium and magnesium) and within 24 hrs mummifies.
- ☆ Larvae unlike other diseases do not rot or decay but remain hard.
- ☆ The entire body except the head becomes covered with white powdery material and the larvae look like dry white stick.
- ☆ During pupal stage, thorax shrinks and abdomen wrinkles. The mummified pupa is hard, lighter and white.
- ☆ During moth stage, the body is hardened and the wings fall off easily.
- ☆ Infected eggs are paler and conidia may be seen on the egg surface. The diseased eggs do not hatch.

Preventive Measures

- ☆ Disinfect the rearing rooms, rearing surroundings

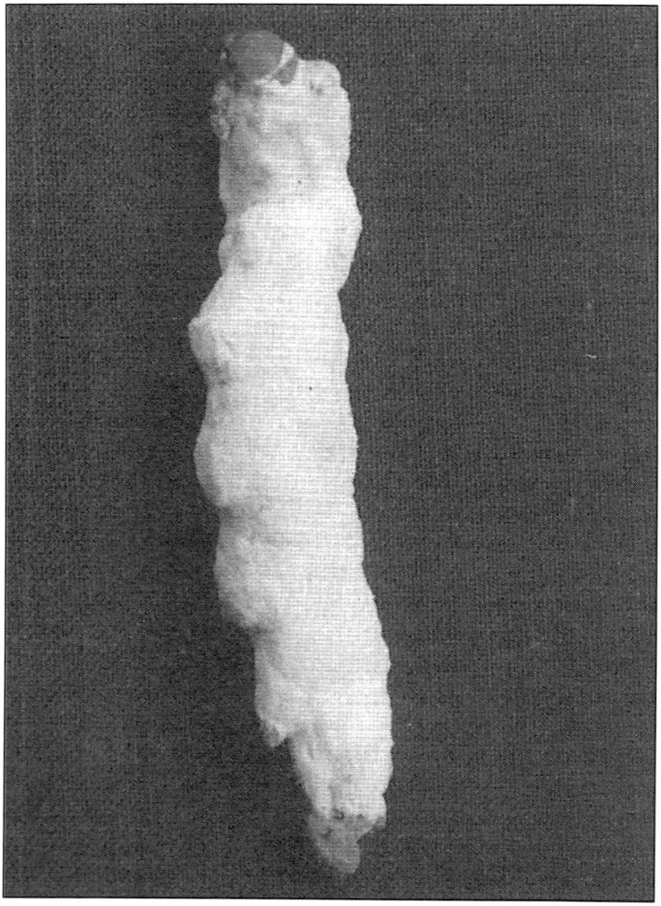

White Muscardine Affected Mummified Silkworm Larvae

and rearing equipments thoroughly before brushing.

☆ Layings are surface sterilized with 2 per cent formalin.

☆ Avoid low temperature and high humidity during rearing.

☆ Provide proper spacing and ventilation.

- ✰ Keep bed dry and thin to avoid germination of spores.
- ✰ Change infected trays and seat paper.
- ✰ Remove diseased larvae before mummification.
- ✰ Destruction of diseased material.
- ✰ Use anti-muscardine agents/bed disinfectant like Labex, Formalin chaff and Dithane M45 or Captan with lavigated china clay (Kaolin) for prevention of the disease.

Formalin Chaff Application

For preparation of formalin chaff paddy husk is charred or burnt either by roasting or burning without making ash. Depending on the stage of larvae, the required strength of formalin (I and II instars–0.4 per cent, III instars–0.5 per cent, IV instars–0.6 per cent and V instars–0.8 per cent) is mixed with the burnt paddy husk in the ratio of 1:10 by volume and mixed thoroughly. The mixture is sprinkled evenly on the larvae, which are then covered with paraffin paper. After half an hour, the paraffin paper is removed and feeding is given. Application can be done after each moult but half an hour before the resumption of the feed. If the incidence is very high, it is applied everyday after bed cleaning. When the larvae settle for moult and are under moult, application of formalin chaff should be avoided. As a precautionary measure, during winter and rainy seasons when there is possibility of occurrence of muscardine in-spite of the earlier muscardine free crops, the application of formalin chaff should be done once in each stage *viz.*, before brushing, after I, II, II and IV moult and on 4th day of 5th instar.

Dithane M-45 or Captan Application

Dithane M–45 and Captan are the two commonly available fungicides used for the control of Muscardine in combination with levigated china clay at the concentration of 1 per cent during I, II and III instars and 2 per cent during IV and V instars. The mixture is dusted on newly born larvae and also after each moult half an hour before the resumption of feed. The quantity required is 2–3 gm/100 sq.cm areas during I, II and III instars and 4–5 gm during IV and V instars. It should not be dusted when the larvae are either in mould or in feeding stage. After dusting, the bed need not be covered with paraffin paper. Feeding should be given after half an hour of dusting.

(*ii*) Green Muscardine

Causative Agent

The green muscardine disease in silkworm is caused by hyphomycetes fungi *Nomuraea rileyi* and *Spicaria prasina* belonging to family Moniliaceae of the division Eumycota, sub-division Deuteromycotina, class Hyphomycetes and order Moniliales.

Route of Infection

Infection takes place through skin by conidia. This disease occurs during autumn, late autumn and winter seasons. The three growth stages of pathogen consist of conidium, vegetative mycelium and aerial mycelium as in white muscardine. The conidium is oval in shape and slightly pointed at one end. It is light green and single celled. It germinates at 20-24°C in 20 hrs. The germinating tube of vegetative mycelium elongates and gives rise to fine and filamentous mycelia. These mycelia produce large number of colorless bean shaped hyphae, which later forms conidiophores. These conidiophores are wheeling shaped and un-branched, which bear few or several sterigmata each of which carries at the tip a chain of conidia.

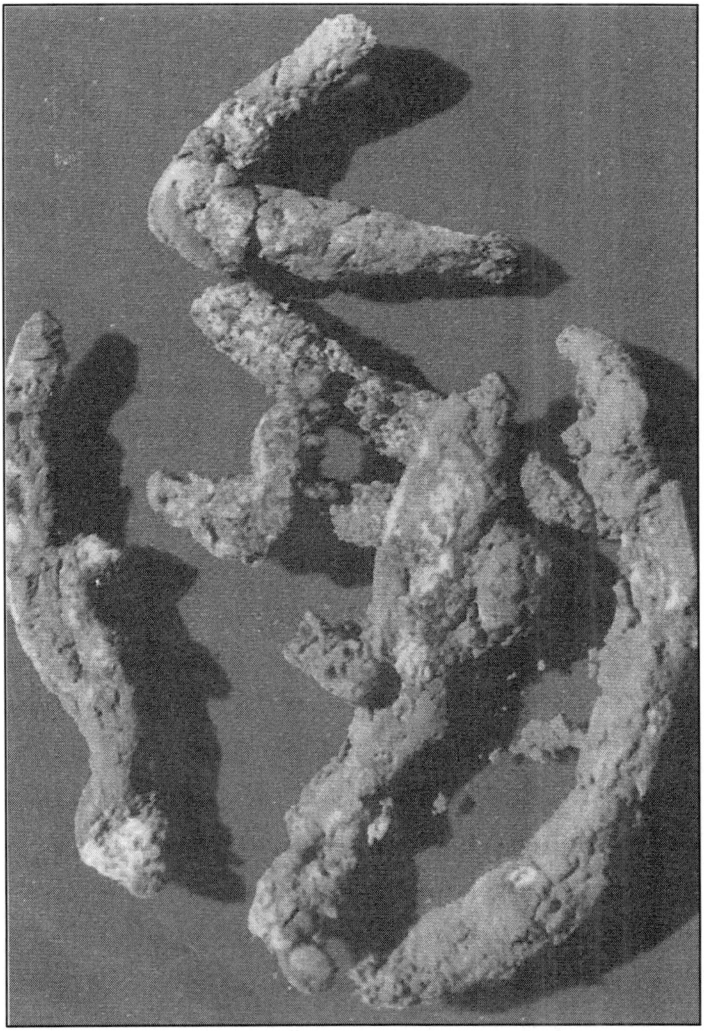

Green Muscardine Affected Mummified Silkworm Larvae

Symptoms

- ☆ Initially, the dead body of the larva appears white in color.
- ☆ Dark brown irregular lesions appear on the ventral, dorsal and lateral sides.
- ☆ In serious case the silkworm vomits fluid, has diarrhoea and dies.
- ☆ After death the soft corpse gradually hardens.
- ☆ Initially the whole body covered with white mycelia.
- ☆ After 10–15 days these white mycelia produce fresh green conidia and worm looks green.
- ☆ The entire body, except the head, will be covered with green powdery material and the larvae look like dry green stick.
- ☆ Infected pupa the thoracic region appears shrunk and the abdomen wrinkled. The pupae are hard, lighter, mummified and greenish color.

Preventive Measures

Prevention and control measures are similar to that of white muscardine.

(iii) Yellow Muscardine

This disease is caused by the infection of yellow Muscardine fungus *Isaria farinosus* or *Paecilomyces farinosus*. It affects both young and late stage larvae. Their death rate is very high particularly during 5th instars and mounting or during cocooning. The symptoms of this disease are more or less same as of white Muscardine except the formation of large number of yellow conidiophores. The spores are oval or spherical in shape. The incidence of disease is greater during autumn.

(*iv*) Black Muscardine

The disease is caused by the infection of *Oospora destructor* or *Beauveria brongniartti* or *Metarrhizium anisopliae.* Its incidence compared to other Muscardine disease is much lower. This disease occurs mainly during hot summer and autumn silkworm rearing. Symptoms are same as in white Muscardine except formation of large number of black conidiophores leading to black appearance of the diseased larvae.

(*v*) Brown Muscardine

This is known to be caused by more than 10 species of the genus *Aspergillus.* Most of these fungi are distributed in the environment. They are saprophytic and become pathogenic only when conditions are favorable. Aspergillosis caused by fungus *Aspergllius* called brown muscardine. Young larvae are very much susceptible to this and die within 2–3 days of infection. Conidiophores are greenish-yellow mixed with brown. It is capable of growing and producing spores even on rearing equipments, walls and floors of rearing rooms besides moist chopping board. All these materials should be disinfected thoroughly to check the occurrence of this disease.

(*vi*) Aspergillosis

One of the fungal diseases infecting silkworm is *Aspergillus* sp. *Aspergillus* species causing aspergillosis of silkworm have been extensively studied, as they are also capable of infecting plants, animals, leather materials, storage grains, animal feeds and dairy products in addition to being pathogenic to a variety of insects. The disease is prevalent in young instar larvae during high humidity conditions. The fungi responsible for the disease are included in Aspergillus and Sterigmatocystis group belonging to the family Moniliaceae of class Fungi Imperfecti. *Aspergillus flavus, A. sojae, A. parasiticus, A. fiavipes, A. nidulans, A. melleus, A. fumigates, A. etegans, A. niger, A. oryzae* and *A. ochraceus* are pathogenic to silkworm.

Classification

Anamorphic stage classification (Domsch *et al.*, 1980)

Kingdom	:	Fungi
Division	:	Eumycota
Sub-division	:	Deuteromycotina
Class	:	Ascomycetes
Order	:	Eurotiales
Family	:	Eurotiaceae
Genus	:	*Aspergillus*

Though Aspergilli's are saprophytic, they are reported to be pathogenic to several insects in addition to *B. mori* (Table 3.4). More than 15 species of *Aspergillus* are identified infecting mulberry silkworm, out of which *A. flavus, A. oryzae, A. tamri* are prominent. Patil (1989) reported *A. flavus* on *B. mori* from India. Freshly hatched larvae are the most susceptible to these fungi. With the larval development, the resistance of the larvae gradually decreases and the resistance is higher during the peak growth period of 5th instars. Thereafter, it once decreases again soon after pupation. Silkworms are very susceptible to these fungal infections. Usually the susceptibility increases with the increase in humidity. When the humidity is 70 per cent, the disease is rare but as the humidity increases, the incidence of disease also increase. The favorable temperature for germination of conidia is 30–35°C. Infected larvae stops eating of mulberry leaf, becomes lethargic, show body tension, lustrousness and then die. Of all the fungi that cause diseases in the silkworm, the conidia of *A. flavus* are the most resistant to environmental factors, being able to survive up to one year or more.

Aspergillus oryzae Disease

This type of aspergillosis is caused by *A. oryzae.* Symptoms of the disease resembles to those of brown muscardine except the formation of spores on the surface, which show light yellow color mixed with dirty brown.

Aspergillus coracles Disease

The disease is very rare compared to other muscardine diseases. The infection level is also very mild. The spores produced are usually orange yellow in color.

Red Muscardine Disease

This type of Aspergillosis is caused by *Isaria fumosorosea.* This fungus has very weak pathogenecity to silkworm. The bodies of the infected worms occasionally show red colored patches a few hours before death. When insect is cut opened, a black red powdery mass of spores is seen. The spore germinates upon exposure to moisture. The parasite destroys the functional organs completely. The 'Kojic acid' has been reported to be produced by *Aspergillus oryzae, A. flavus, A. candidus, A. fumigatus, A. giganteus, A.niger.* There is close relationship among Kojic acid production, resistance to formalin and virulence to the silkworm larvae. The isolate with a high productivity of kojic acid showed a high resistance to formalin and severe virulence to silkworm larvae.

Table 3.4: Lepidopteron Host Range of *Aspergillus* sp. Pathogenic to Silkworm and Reported from India

Name of Insect	Pest on	References
A] ***Aspergillus flavus***		
Nephantis serinopa	Coconut palm	Oblisami *et al.* (1969)
Azogophieps scalaris	Sesbania	Oblisami *et al.* (1969)
Amsacta albistriga	Groundnut	Oblisami *et al.* (1969)
Utethesia pulchella	Sun hemp	Oblisami *et al.* (1969)
Achoea janata	Castor	Oblisami *et al.* (1969)
Euproctis fraternal	Plum	Batra & Sinha (1971)
Parasa lepida	Coconut	Pillai & Ayyar (1969)
Spilosoma oblique	Agricultural crops	Battu *et al.* (1971)
Spodoptera litura	Agricultural crops	Battu *et al.* (1971)
Pelopidas mathias	Rice	Veluswamy *et al.* (1973)
Chilo parteilus	Maize and Sorghum	Atwal *et al.* (1973)
Lymantria obfuscata	Cacao	Nair & Premkumar (1974)
B] ***A. parasiticus***		
Drosicha magniferae	Citrus and Mango	Saxena & Rawatt (1968)
C] ***A. candidus***		
Indarbela sp.	Guava and Plum	Singh & Singh (1984)
Utethesia pulchella	Crotalaria	Mathur *et al.* (1970)
D] ***Aspergillus tamarii***		
Azygophleps scalaris	Sesbania	Sithanantham (1970)
Dasychria menctosa	Mulberry	Chinnaswamy *et al.* (1986)
E] ***Aspergillus nidulans***		
Samia cynthia ricini	Eri	Devaiah *et al.* (1982-83)

The rapid development of fungus, *Aspergillus* is due to the nutrition and suitable environment like high temperature and high humidity. Winter and rainy seasons are favorable for the incidence of aspergillosis due to high relative humidity in the environment. Sporadic incidence of *Aspergillus* is also reported during summer at high temperature and high humidity. High humidity (80-85 per cent) influences the growth of *Aspergillus* species, even at the high temperature level because this fungus can withstand and survive up to the temperature of 40°C in combination with high RH.

Preventive Measures

- ✰ Dilthiocarbamate fungicides are found effective for bed disinfections. Also disinfections by organosulfurous fungicides such as 2 per cent Maneb, 2 per cent Zineb and 2 per cent Mancozeb resulted in above 90 per cent survival of silkworm larvae.
- ✰ Bavistin, Bayleton, Vitavax, Dithane M–45, Daconil and formalin are found controlling the aspergillosis of silkworm.
- ✰ Disinfection of rearing rooms and equipments with 0.5 per cent Pentachlorophenol in addition to general disinfection with formalin and bleaching powder.
- ✰ Avoid high humidity in rearing bed.
- ✰ Maintain optimum spacing and bed thickness during rearing.
- ✰ Diseased material, faeces should be destroyed or piled into the compost pit to kill the germs.

- ☆ Hygiene management in and around the silkworm rearing house and also by the persons handing the silkworms.
- ☆ Dusting of 0.5 per cent Chlite after moult (Chlite is similar to bleaching powder).
- ☆ So far many silkworm breed have been screened for their susceptibility to *A. flavus* and *A. tamarii.* It is a boon to tropics that multivoltine genotypes are less susceptible to *Aspergillus* compared to bivoltine as the former are usually used as maternal parents in hybrid egg production.

Methods to Manage High Temperature and Low Humidity

- ☆ Avoid rearing house with asbestos or tin roof.
- ☆ Raise shade trees around the rearing house, cover the roof with coconut thatches, grass or palm leaves.
- ☆ Apply 'Cool Guard' to the roof top.
- ☆ Feed mulberry leaves with higher moisture content. Harvest mulberry leaves during cooler hours, sprinkle water and preserve them in dark and cooler area.
- ☆ Keep windward windows and floor level ventilators closed during hot period of the day.
- ☆ Provide wet gunny cloth curtain to the windows and doors.
- ☆ Wipe floor with water during day time once at 11 AM and again at 3 PM.
- ☆ Increase the frequency of feeding from 2-3 to 3-4 times a day.

- ☆ Feed reduced quantity of leaves during noon and more during night.
- ☆ During hot period, cover the bed with old newspaper, after feeding.

Methods to Manage Low Temperature and High Humidity

- ☆ Regulate air circulation without causing suffocation.
- ☆ Use heaters (electrical or charcoal) to raise room temperature.
- ☆ Dust dry slaked lime powder on the rearing room floor.
- ☆ Dust dry slaked lime powder on the silkworms, after bed cleaning or before feeding in the morning.
- ☆ Avoid over feeding. Feed only the quantum of mulberry leaves, the larvae consumes during the feed period.
- ☆ Avoid accumulation of silkworm waste and faeces in the bed.
- ☆ Feed comparatively more mature leaves than the leaves fed during normal period.

[4] Protozoan Disease

The mulberry silkworm, *Bombyx mori,* is prone to infections of various pathogenic organisms. Microsporidiosis of the silkworm caused by highly virulent parasitic microsporidian, *Nosema bombycis* (Nageli) is one of the most serious maladies, which determines the success or failure of sericulture industry in any country. Infections of the disease range from chronic to highly virulent and can result in heavy loss to sericulture industry. Several strains and species of microsporidians have since been isolated from the infected silkworms; the disease is becoming increasingly more and more complex. Epizootiology, development of immunodiagnostic kit, fluorescent antibody technique and use of ideal disinfectant, chemotherapy and thermo-therapy techniques and management strategies has been addressed for identification, destruction, prevention and control of disease causing microorganisms. Technique of forced eclosion test and delayed mother moth examination also plays an important role in the detection of the disease and to harvest stable cocoon crop. In this Chapter efforts have been made to present annotated information on the causative organism, pathogenesis, manifestation, diagnosis and management of microsporidia infecting mulberry silkworm, *Bombyx mori*.

Pebrine disease of silkworm is a disastrous disease which ensures success, or failure of sericulture industry in any country. This is a chronic insidious disease, evidenced by the historical fact that the rise and fall of the pebrine disease corresponds with ups and downs of the sericulture industry in silk producing countries of the world. At one time or the other, it has severely damaged sericulture in all the silk producing countries of the world. The evidence showed that the pebrine outbreak started in France during 1845. France total production, which had reached 26,000,000 kg in 1853, fell to only 4,000,000 kg in 1865. During this time the disease was so rampant that sericulture in France was on the verge of collapse (Tatsuke, 1971). The history of research on pebrine disease progressed with the advancement of microbiology in 19th century. The name 'pebrine' was coined by De Quadrefages (1860) because of the appearance of pepper-like spots in the diseased larvae. The disease-causing microorganism was first observed in haemolymph of silkworms and was given the name 'Hematozoid' (Guerin–Menaville, 1849). Later Nageli of Germany stated that the disease is caused by a protozoan parasite and named this pathogen, *Nosema bombycis.* Louis Pasteur called the disease as 'Corpuscles disease', made a detailed study on its growth and transmission, discovered that disease is contracted through transovam transmission within the body of mother moth, and suggested the method of preventing the disease. Balblain made it known that the pathogen of pebrine disease belongs to Protozoa. Later on in 1909, Stempell published the detailed of his study on the life history of the pathogen of pebrine disease. Based on the microsporidians unusual cytological and molecular characteristics such as primitive type of nuclear division, devoid of mitochondria, prokaryotic sized ribosome's and ribosomal RNAs, they have been phylogenetically considered as one of the earliest known eukaryotes (Vossbrinck *et al.*, 1987).

In India, the first record of spread of incidence of disease was at the end of the 19th Century in Kashmir valley. In 1890-1900, the disease swept through Mysore and Madras province. Thereafter, the disease reappeared during 1925-1930 in an epizootic form (Chitra *et al.*, 1975). Disease epidemics were again observed during 1991-1992 which resulted in considerable crop loss and revenue of over 200 crores during the period. Since then the incidence of the disease is being observed intermittently in silkworm crops in different parts of India. The microsporidia are spore forming, small, obligate, intracellular living eukaryote infecting both beneficial and non-beneficial insects

(Nataraju *et al.*, 2005). More than 140 genera and 1200 species of microsporidians are recorded from insects and fishes (Canning, 1993, Samson *et al.*, 1999a). Among them at least 200 belongs to the genus *Nosema* (Sprague, 1982) and most *Nosema* species are parasitic to invertebrates. A majority of these such as *N. bombycis* and *N. tyriae* (Canning *et al.*, 1999), *N. mesnili* (Cheung and Wang, 1995), *N. algerae* (Muller *et al.*, 2000), *N. aphis* and *N. trichoplusiae* (Malone *et al.*, 1994) are pathogenic to various insects. The microsporidian infection remains a major threat to sericulture industry with its recurrent occurrence. More than twenty wild insect species are found to have microsporidian spores that can cross-infect silkworm. Pebrine, the spores of microsporidian (*Nosema bombycis)* is one of the most dreaded diseases of the silkworm, *Bombyx mori*. Pebrine infects almost all ages, stages, breeds and hybrids of the silkworm by both transovarial and peroral infection. It is highly infectious and difficult to eradicate after the occurrence of infection. The earliest research on pebrine was confined especially with the epizootiology and prevention of the disease (Weiser, 1969; Ishihara, 1963; Fujiwara, 1979). Microscopical method of mother moth examination, although widely practiced mainly due to its simplicity, does not assure full-proof detection of the microsporidian.

To circumvent this problem efforts have been made to evolve simple, precise and more accurate method of detection of the disease (Geethabai *et al.*, 1985; Fujiwara, 1993; Baig *et al.*, 1992; Shi and Jin, 1997), identification of alternate host (Fujiwara, 1993; Samson, 2000), use of chemotherapy and thermo-therapy for the prevention and control of disease (Hayasaka, 1990) besides identification of intermediary stages (Santha *et al.*, 2001) but with little success. Even though, the researches and fight against the pebrine has been continuing for more than a century, loss due to disease has not been eliminated completely. However, historical evidences suggest a significant relationship between success of sericulture industry and the control of the disease. Therefore, for the improvement of sericulture industry and to save it from the crop losses caused due to this chronic nature of the disease, it is essential to have a full-proof diagnostic and preventive technique.

Systematic Position

Phylum	:	Protozoa
Sub-phylum	:	Cnidospora
Class	:	Sporozoa
Sub-class	:	Neosporidia
Order	:	Microsporidia
Sub-order	:	Monocnidina
Family	:	Nosematidae
Genus	:	*Nosema*
Species	:	*bombycis* (N.)

Pathogen

Several microsporidians are known to cause the disease in silkworm. Among them the most common are *Nosema bombycis* and strains of *Nosema* sp., NIK-2r, NIK-3h, NIS-001, NIS-M11, NIS-M14), *Vermimorpha* (NIS-M12 and NIK-4m), *Pleistophora* sp. (NIS-M27), *Thelohania* (NIS-M32) and *Leptomonas* sp.

Life Cycle of *Nosema bombycis*

The life cycle of *Nosema bombycis* (Nageli) includes three stages namely, spore, planont and meront. Mature spore is oval or ovocylindrical and measures 3–4 microns by 1.5 - 2.0 microns with three-layered membrane, the inner, middle and outer. They can be observed at 600 magnifications under a microscope. The spores consists of:

- ☆ Spore membrane, which encloses the sporoplasm.
- ☆ Sporoplasm in the form of a girdle across the width of the spore.
- ☆ Anterior and posterior vacuoles.
- ☆ Two nuclei in the sporoplasm.
- ☆ Posterior capsule.

The spores are highly refractive, appearing light green under the microscope. The outline is smooth and the spores are heavier than the water. The spore belongs to the dormant stage of pathogen and possesses great resistance. For example, they can remain infective after three years in the dried body of the female moth and remain active after being sub-merged in water for five month. The spore germinates in digestive juice of silkworm larva and produces a long polar filament having a length of more than 30 times that of the lengthwise dimension of the spore, on the end of which grows a sporoplasm (germs). The sporoplasm is having two nuclei and other cell organs and possesses the limiting membrane. The sporoplasm multiplies through fission, comes out of the haemolymph through intracellular spaces spreading to every part of the body, and lives in various systems particularly in the fat body and muscular tissue, becomes a nucleus and form spore after multiplication through fission. Spore formation is apansporoblastic, disporous and dimorphic. One type of sporoblast of the long polar tube type turns into single spore and many coil of polar tube. The other type is the sporoblast of the short polar tube, which turns into single spore with few coils of polar tube. Spores of short polar tube hatches directly in the host cell. The mature spore is unicellular endomembranous differentiation of its sporoblast. The pathogen of pebrine disease is capable to complete its life cycle within 4 days. The pathogen parasitizes the ovary first and when 4th or 5th instar larvae after pupation and emergence becomes moth they move into egg and after deposition of eggs undergo multiplication and develops into a disease in the embryo or in the body of silkworm in next generation. After the deposition of eggs the pathogen grows and multiplies within the egg. The mature spore is unicellular endo-membranous differentiation of its sporoblast (Vavra and Maddox, 1976). These authors designated the sporoblasts as Phase-I sporoblasts and Phase-II sporoblasts. The Phase-I sporoblasts are characterized by the presence of a dark staining spherical body.

Source and Stage of Contamination

Transversally infected seeds are the primary source of contamination. Contaminated seed crop rearing and grainage buildings, appliances, silkworm litter, mulberry leaf fed to the silkworm harbored by infected insects etc also contributes to the spread of the disease. The incidence of pebrine varies with the breeds/hybrids of silkworm, the developmental stage and the rearing environment. Resistance to pebrine is greater in Chinese breeds, less in Japanese and least in European breeds (Govindan *et al.*,

1998) and that multivoltine breeds are relatively more resistant than bivoltines (Patil and Geethabai, 1989). Young silkworms, newly moulted and starving larvae are susceptible and show high mortality. In India, Nistari and C. Nichi silkworm breeds are more resistant compared to others. Patil and Geethabai (1989) reported that among bivoltines breeds NB7 is most susceptible followed by NB4D2, KA and NB18. Although the disease resistance appears to depend on the genetic constituents of a particular breed, nevertheless factors such as pathogen load, inadequate nutrition and the environment in which insects are reared may also affect resistance (Patil, 1993). In addition, the physical and physiological characteristics of hosts may make the invasion of microsporidians possible (Weiser, 1969, 1977). The larvae infected during 1st and 2nd instars show normal growth up to 3rd instars. Disease symptoms appear during later half of 4th instars to first half of 5th instars and die before spinning. If the contamination takes place in 3rd instars, the larvae show symptoms of the disease in the late 5th instars and die on the mountage before cocooning. These larvae discharge spores through faecal matter during 4th and 5th instars. If these larvae are reared with healthy larvae, the spore discharge by infected larvae provides the source of contamination and digestion of spores by healthy silkworms results in spread of the disease. This stage of contamination is known as 'second stage of contamination'. Larvae infected during 4th and 5th instars pupate and on emergence lay contaminated eggs. This phenomenon is referred as 'transovarian transmission'. Most of the larvae infected through transovarian transmission show irregular moulting and growth, becomes tiny or under grown and die before 3rd moult after discharging spores. The contamination occurring from transovarially-infected larvae is termed as 'first stage of contamination'. The minimum number of spores required for contamination through per oral infection varies with each instar. Iwano and Ishihara (1981) stated that 1–10 spores are sufficient to cause disease in 2nd instars larvae, while approximately 100 such spores are required in 5th instars for the same symptoms to occur. Transovarian transmission is 100 per cent in case of *N. bombycis* and only 1.2 per cent with *Nosema* sp. M11 (Han and Watanabe, 1988).

The spores of different microsporidia infecting silkworms differ in their morphological characters, some are larger than mature spore and some are long, thin and pear-shaped with different size, shape and luster. Sometimes the conidia of green muscardine and red muscardine bear a striking resemblance to the spore of pebrine disease. Horizontal transmission of pebrine spore is possible through contaminated rearing bed, contaminated mulberry leaf and through contaminated layings (Govindan *et al.*, 1998). Baig *et al.* (1988a) reported that spread of disease in rearing trays is also dependent on the density of diseased silkworms. Growth and multiplication of pathogen are influenced by growth of its host. When egg enters into diapause, the growth and multiplication of pathogen stops simultaneously and when egg starts growing, the pathogen also starts growing and multiplying.

Cross Infectivity

Different species of insects known to carry microsporidians causing cross-infectivity to silkworms are found harboring in and around mulberry garden. Enormous quantity of microsporidian spores is observed in *Catopsilia* sp., an inhabitant of mulberry garden (Kishore *et al.*, 1994) and found infective to silkworms. Butterflies causing microsporidian infections to silkworms are also reported (Samson *et al.*, 1999a, b). Singh *et al.* (2007) reported that butterflies *i.e Eurena hecabae* and *Zizina otis* carry microsporidian spores infective to silkworms. These insects are potential source of contamination as spores of pathogen is excreted along with litter on mulberry leaves in the garden and when these leaves are fed to silkworms, they causes the disease to appear.

Physiological Stability

Generally, large number of factors *viz.*, temperature, humidity and abiotic components of the substrate influence the survival of microsporidians (Kramer, 1976). The spores belong to the dormant stage of pathogen and possess great resistance, can remain infective after 3 years in the dried body of the female moth, and become active after being submerged in water (Li, 1985). When kept in dark, the spores are reported to remain viable for as long as seven years, but when spores are directly exposed to sunshine (Anonymous, 1980) they remain viable for 6–7 hrs and when treated with hot water survive for just 5 minutes. Studies conducted on the viability of pebrine spores in soil and compost under tropical conditions showed survival of spores for maximum period of 225 days in wet soil and minimum of 135 days in wet compost (Patil, 1993). Srikanta (1986) observed that spores remained infective even after 150 days of refrigeration and after 90 days in moist soil and faeces. He further stated that the viability of spores is lost in 60 days in dry soil and in 5 days when stored at room temperature. Resistance of spores to different disinfectants indicates that it can remain viable for 10–30 minutes in the solution of corrosive sublimate, for about 5 hrs in formalin and 10 hrs in chlorinated lime solution (diluted 10,000 times). Bleaching powder containing 1 per cent and 3 per cent active chlorine can render spore inactive in 30 minutes and 10 minutes respectively. When the degree of infection is relatively high, the egg often becomes sterile or dead, but when the contamination is of low degree, the egg hatches and the disease develops at larval stage and caused death of larvae at later stages of development. The growth and multiplication of pathogen in the eggs are influenced by the growth of the host. When the egg diapauses, the growth and multiplication of the pathogen stops simultaneously and when the eggs start growing by incubation, the pathogen also starts growing and multiplying.

Alternate Hosts

Most microsporidians prefer to have alternate hosts because of many advantages for them *viz.*, dispersal, transmission and survival. The perpetual incidence of microsporidian infection in silkworms may be due to various sources of secondary contaminations including alternate hosts in and around mulberry garden. In addition to *N. bombycis*, seven other microsporidians belonging to the genera *Nosema, Pleistophora, Thelohania, Vairomorpha* and *Leptomonas* spp. has been isolated from the silk moth (Govindan *et al.*, 1998). They differ in their spore morphology, target tissue and virulence and have been designated as M11, M12 and M14 (*Nosema* sp.), M24, M25, M27 (*Pleistophora* sp.) (Fuziwara, 1984a & b) and M32 (*Thelohania* sp.) (Fujiwara, 1985) (Table 3.5). Three microsporidians designated as NIK-2r, NIK-3h and NIK-4m have been isolated from Karnataka (India) and these

Table 3.5: Different types of *Nosema* spores

Microsporidian	*Spore Size (μm)*	*Site of Infection*	*Virulence*	*Shape*
Nosema bombycis	3.8 x 2.2	Systemic	High	Oval
Nosema sp. (M11)	3.9 x 1.9	Various tissues	Low	Cylindrical
Nosema sp. (M12)	4.2 x 2.7	Various tissues	Low	Cylindrical
Nosema sp. (M14)	5.1 x 2.0	Various tissues	High	Cylindrical
Pleistophora sp. (M24)	2.7 x 1.6	Mid gut	Low	Oval
Pleistophora sp. (M25)	3.2 x 1.8	Mid gut	Low	Oval
Pleistophora sp. (M27)	5.4 x 3.0	Various tissues	Low	Oval
Thelohania sp. (M32)	3.4 x 1.7	Muscle	Low	Oval
Nosema sp. NIK-Is	3.8 x 2.6	Various tissues	High	Oval
Nosema sp. NIK-2r	3.6 x 2.8	Various tissues	High	Round
Nosema sp. NIK-3h	3.8 x 1.8	Various tissues	Low	Oval
Varimorpha sp. NIK-4m	5.0 x 2.1	Gut	High	Ovocylindrical

are immunologically dissimilar to *N. bombycis* (Ananthalakshmi *et al.*, 1994).

N. bombycis is also reported to infect *Samia Cynthia ricini* and Indian tropical tasar, muga and Chinese tasar silkworms (Talukdar, 1980). *N. bombycis* is also found to infect a several other lepidopterans like *Spodoptera exigua, S. litura, Diaphania pulvurentalis, Pieris rapae, P. brassicae* etc. Veber (1958) reported 32 species of lepidopterans known to develop infection to the peroral inoculation of *N. bombycis* spores. They include *Chilo suppressalis, Pieris rapae, P. brassicae, Spodoptera exigua, S. litura, S. maurilia, Balataea funeralis, Cruptophlebia illepida, Exartema mori, E. morivirum, Diaphania pyloalis, Mycalesis gotoma, Abracus miranda, Descorba simplex, Boarmia selenlia, Menophra atrilinecta, Elydna nonagrica, Otosema odera, Perigea illecta, Plusia chalcites, Pseudaletia unipuncta, Stilpnotia lubricipeda, S. imparilis, Callimorpha quadripunctata, Thaumetopoea processionea, Malacosoma neustria, Gastropacha quercifolia, Lasiocampa quercus, Bombyx mandarina, Antheraea pernyi, A. yamamai, Sphinx ligustris, Agrotis ipsilon, Agrius cinagulatus, Pholera assimilis, Acronicta major, Acrotomycis aceris* and *Achaea janata* (Samson *et al.*, 1999b; Kawarabata, 2003; Singh *et al.*, 2007, 2010). The lawn grass cutworm, *Spodoptera depravata* serves as a natural reservoir for the pathogen (Ishihara and Iwano, 1991), which shares the surface specific antigens with *N. bombycis* and results in transovarial transmission with less virulence.

Epidemiology

Source of Infection

The source of pebrine infections are many including diseased larvae and wild insects affected by the diseases, excreta and faeces, urine of the ripe larvae and moths, discarded eggshells, pupal skin and scales, epicuticle and cocoon shell.

Routes of Infection

Nosema sp. transmits infection both vertically and horizontally in the silkworm. The primary infection is by vertical transmission with the pathogen transferring the infection directly from the parent to the offspring's or by horizontal transmission where the transmission is by secondary infection from one individual to another which is accompanied by ingestion of spores. These two types can also be termed as oral and transovarian transmission. Orally eating mulberry leaves contaminated by pathogen infects silkworm. Trans-ovarian transmission occurs when the pebrine pathogen infects the 4th and 5th instars larvae and then invades the epithelial cells of the ovaries, from where the parasites are transferred to the oogonia, oocytes and nutritive cells. Parasitism of the oocytes results in the death of the eggs. The result of the embryonic infection, however, differs according to the stage when invasion of the embryos occurs. If infection takes place during the formation of embryos, then no embryonic development takes place and the eggs die.

Transmission within the rearing tray is caused by sick silkworms in which large quantities of pebrine spores formed are excreted with the faeces or attaches to epicuticles, thus contaminating the rearing tray and transmitting the disease to the healthy worms. Infection inside the rearing tray may be divided into two categories *i.e* primary and secondary contamination. Primary contamination refers to that occurring in the 1st and 2nd instar and the excretion of spores taking place in the 3rd or 4th instars. Ingestion of these spores by other healthy larvae constitutes secondary contamination. Secondary contaminated silkworms are able to feed normally and become adult moths but they lay infected eggs. Young silkworms infected in the 1st or 2nd instars usually die in the 3rd instars but rarely in 4th instars. If infection occurs in 4th instars, development may proceed to the adult stage with laying of eggs but the eggs laid will be infected with pebrine. Young silkworms freshly moulted and starving larvae are more susceptible to the disease and show high mortality. The spread of pebrine infection is generally by secondary contaminations.

Symptoms of the Disease

The disease symptoms depend on the parasitism of the metamorphic stage. The symptoms of the disease can be observed in all the stages of silkworm development *viz.*, egg, larva, pupa and moth.

Symptoms in Egg Stage

- ☆ Poor egg number.
- ☆ Pilling of eggs one over the other.
- ☆ Lack of adhesive fluid and poor adherence to the egg sheet.
- ☆ Lack of uniformity in egg shape.
- ☆ More unfertilized and dead eggs.
- ☆ Poor and irregular hatching.

Symptoms in Larval Stage

- ☆ Larvae show poor appetite.
- ☆ Retarded growth and development leading to un-uniformity in size (unequal larvae).

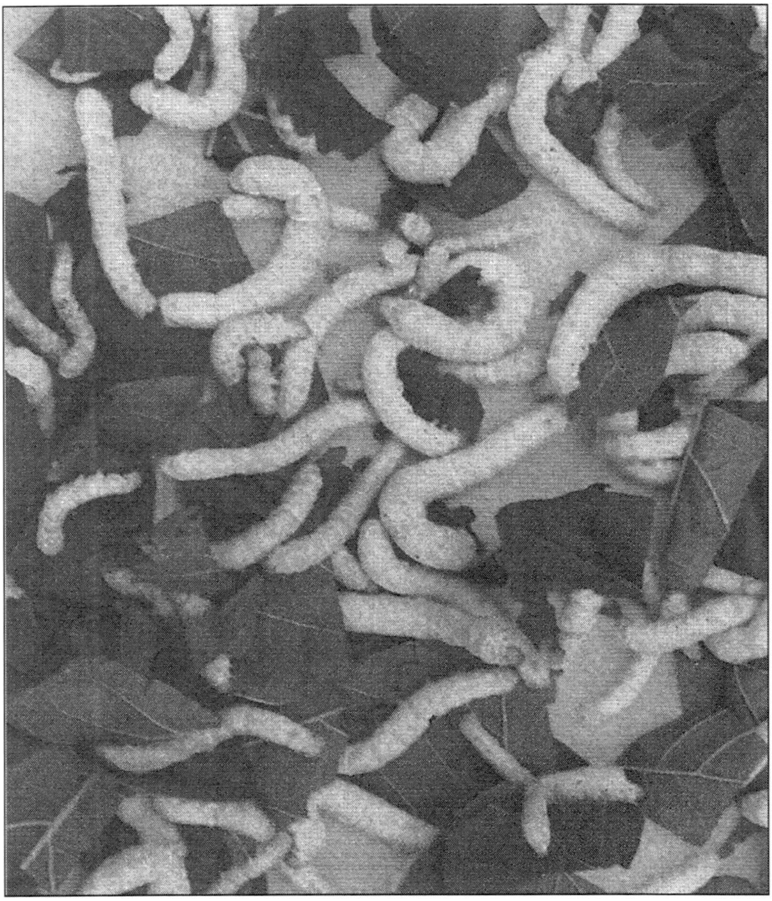

Size Variation in Pebrine Affected Silkworm Larvae

- Larvae show altered colour, size and activity.
- Diseased larvae are comparatively paler and translucent.
- Larvae moult irregularly and show sluggishness.
- Body shows wrinkled skin.

- ☆ They lose appetite, retard in growth, sometimes vomit gut juice, shrink in size and become undersized.
- ☆ The affected gut becomes opaque and the silk gland shows white pustules in different places along its length.
- ☆ Sometimes black irregular pepper like spots on the skin.
- ☆ Irregular and incomplete moulting.
- ☆ The dead larvae remain rubbery for longer period and then turn black.

Symptoms in Pupal Stage

- ☆ Pupae are flabby and swollen with lusterless and softened abdomen.
- ☆ Irregular black spots appear near the rudiments of the wing and abdominal area.
- ☆ Highly infected pupae fail to metamorphose as adult moth.

Symptoms in the Moth Stage

- ☆ Delayed and irregular/erratic moth emergence.
- ☆ Clubbed wings with distorted antennae.
- ☆ The diseases moths will be inactive and do not mate properly.
- ☆ Scales from the wings and abdominal area easily falls-off.
- ☆ Clumpy egg laying.

Spore Isolation and Purification

Isolation, purification and identification of spores from the host are the first step in the study of pebrine disease and its management. Following centrifugal procedure (Fujiwara's method) of microscopical examination is carried out for spore isolation and identification in order to monitor the disease:

- Take 20 larvae/pupae or moth in a cup of domestic mixer.
- Add 80 ml of 0.6 per cent potassium carbonate solution (K_2CO_3).
- Homogenize the larvae/pupae or moth for 1–2 minutes at 10,000 r.p.m. This ensures liberation of spores from the tissues into the medium facilitating more accurate detection of spores during microscopical examination.
- After homogenizing, the contents (homogenate) are transferred into a glass beaker and are allowed to settle for 2–5 minutes. This facilitates to separate host tissues from the liquid portion of homogenate for easy filtration.
- Filter the homogenate by using absorbent cotton or muslin cloth. Volume of filtrate recovered will be around 70 ml.
- Transfer the filtrate into 100 ml capacity of centrifuge tube through funnel. All the centrifuge tubes should be evenly balanced, capped and loaded into the centrifuge machine.
- Centrifugate the filtrate at 3000 r.p.m. for 3–5 minutes to facilitate sedimentation of spores.

- ☆ Remove the centrifuge tube from the centrifuge machine.
- ☆ Discard slowly the supernatant solution.
- ☆ Dissolve the sediment by shaking with a few drops (2–3 drops) of K_2CO_3 or by using a cyclomixer (10–15 seconds) or with a glass rod, which facilitates uniform dissolving.
- ☆ Take this smear from the centrifuge tube on the micro-slide, put the cover slip and examine under 600x magnification of microscope.
- ☆ Minimum 5 microscopic fields should be examined per smear to detect the presence of pebrine spores.

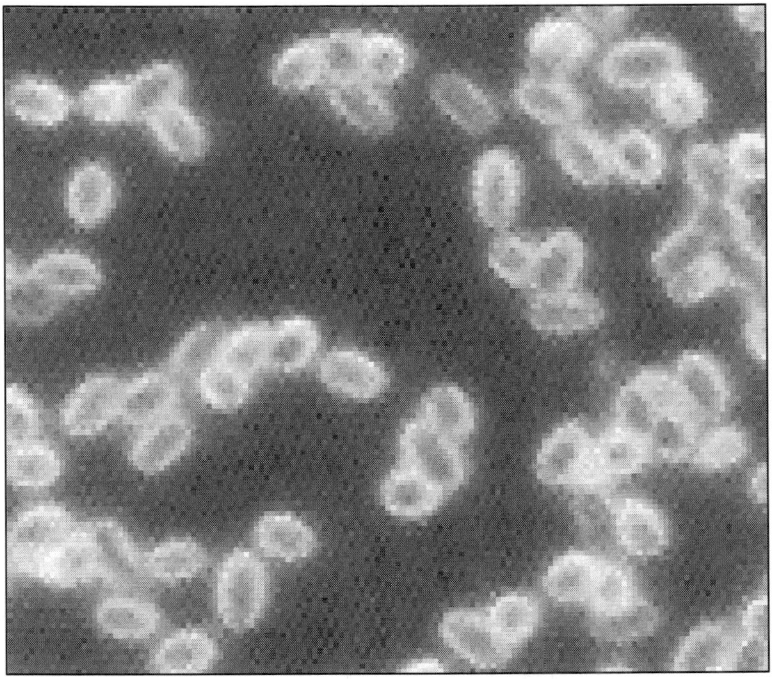

Pebrine Spores Isolated from Silkworm Moth

- ☆ Two moth testers to ensure the detection of pebrine spores may perform microscopical examination.
- ☆ If pebrine spores are detected, the entire batch of eggs laid by the infected mother moths is to be destroyed by burning.
- ☆ The intensity of spores can be graded as below (Table 3.6)

Table 3.6: Intensity of Spores and Pebrine Infection Grading

Number of Spores/Field	*Grade*
1–3	±
4–10	1 +
11–30	2 +
31–100	3 +
101–300	4 +
301–above	∝

However, serological and biochemical studies of microsporidians require high degree of purity. Gochnaner and Margetts (1980) described rapid method for concentrating *Nosema* spores based on continuous flow centrifugation method. Another method based on 'Brownian movement' was also reported. Sato and Watanabe (1980) purified spores using sucrose and percol gradient centrifugation method and reported that centrifugation using percol at 73,000g for 30 minutes resulted in 3 bands:

(*a*) A sharp band consisting of tissues of silkworms, mulberry leaves and bacteria etc.

(*b*) A dim band consisting of mature but inactive spores,

(*c*) Another sharp band consisting of only mature and active spores.

Approaches for Pebrine Prevention and Management

Pebrine has remained a threat to sericulture industry since time immemorial. The disease has become more complex now because of the occurrence of different types of microsporidians infecting the silkworm. Some of them belong to other genera like *Vairomorpha* and *Thelohania* and exhibit differences in their pattern of infection (Samson, *et al.*, 1999a). Apparently, the biology of the pathogen has been used as a basis in disease control. The disease is transmitted horizontally by ingestion of spore and vertically by transovarian transmission. This unique characteristic of the disease made difficult to completely eliminate it from the silkworm crops. The earliest method suggested by Pasteur based on selection of pathogen free eggs through careful systematic examination of mother moths for pathogens, after egg laying has been one of the most effective methods even today to avoid the disease in the silkworm crops.

Proper monitoring and testing of seed crops at every successive stages of progress of the crop is to be ensured to produce pebrine free seed cocoons for commercial seed production. Destruction of infected crops as soon as noticed infection is another important step towards pebrine disease management. Since the disease is seed borne, the surface sterilization of eggs immediately after egg laying and also before incubation should be followed to prevent disease occurrence from surface contamination (Singh *et al.*, 1992). Several reports documented the efficiency of thermal treatment of silkworm eggs in minimizing pebrine infection

(Bedniakova and Vereiskava, 1958; Fujiwara and Kagawa, 1984; Hayasaka, 1990). The maximum lowering of infection rate is reported in eggs incubated during first two days of their development to 44°C. Singh and Saratchandra (2003) stated that incubation of eggs at higher temperature within 3 days of laying results in significant reduction in pebrine disease. Thermal treatment combined with hydrochlorization to achieve dual objectives of elimination of pebrine and termination of diapause is also reported Liu (1984) achieved remarkable success in reducing pebrine infection after treatment of silkworm eggs at 47°C for 10–20 minutes. Chowdhary (1967) suggested exposure of cocoons to high temperature (33.8°C) at the time of pupation for 16 hrs a day, at 55–65 per cent humidity tends to reduce infection in the resulting eggs. Sheeba *et al.* (1999) reported that thermo-therapy of 7 days old pebrinized cocoons at 36°C for 16 hrs tends to reduce pebrine infection significantly without affecting the growth and development of larvae.

Certain insect hosts tolerate high temperature than their microsporidian parasites and the host can be freed of the disease by rearing the infected individuals at higher temperature until the disease is cured. Attempts have been made by several workers to control pebrine infection in silkworm eggs by temperature treatment. Ovanesyan and Lobzhanidze (1960) and Austrurov *et al.* (1969) attempted hot water treatment of pebrinized eggs and reported sharp decrease in the degree of infection. Smyk (1959) expressed varying success with hot water treatment. Fujiwara and Kagawa (1984) reported that the parasites in non-diapausing eggs are more sensitive to hot water (46°C for 4 minutes) treatment and there is no harmful effect of the treatment on the normal development of silkworm embryos. However, these methods are not effective enough to eliminate infection completely. Chemotherapy of microsporidians infection has been attempted in silkworm. Of the several therapeutic drugs, Benomyl, Nosematol, Bavistin and Thiophanate have been identified as anti-microsporidian agents to control *N. bombycis* infections (Chandra and Sahakundu, 1983 and Alenkseenork, 1986). The toxins of *B. thuringiensis* are also reported efficient in killing the *Nosema* spores. Fumagillin is commonly used to reduce the economic losses due to *Nosema*. Though these methods have proved experimentally effective in reducing the multiplication of spores but further studies has clearly showed that they cannot eliminate transovarian transmission significantly. *N. bombycis* is made to be inactive by hilite (Potassium dichloro isocyanurate) (Iwano and Ishihara, 1981). Baig *et al.* (1988b) studied comparative efficacy of four disinfectants *viz.*, hilite, sodium hypochlorite, bleaching powder and formalin in four concentrations (0.5 per cent, 1 per cent, 1.5 per cent and 2 per cent) as surface sterilents against the spread of pebrine disease in a colony of silkworm hatched from surface contaminated layings and reported that all the tested concentrations were effective in preventing the spread of the disease and were also effective in inactivating spores of *N. bombycis* when exposed to 5, 10, 20 and 30 minutes respectively. Kagawa (1980) studied the efficacy of formalin as disinfectant against pebrine and reported increased death rate of spores with increase in formalin concentration and temperature. Iwano and Ishihara (1981) tested nine types of chemicals as inhibitory agent against *N. bombycis*, with high degree of inhibitory effect on the spores. Treatment of silkworm eggs with HCl of 1.03–1.09 specific gravity at 47°C for 10–20 minutes is known to reduce the disease incidence by 97.4 per cent–100 per cent (Liu and Zhong, 1988). Hot air treatment (48–50°C) of 12–18 hrs old silkworm eggs also inhibited the development of microsporidians. Silkworm eggs of 36–60 hr old treated with hot water at 46°C for 90–150 minutes, 48°C for 50–70 minutes and 52°C for 4 minutes also inhibited the development of pebrine disease.

However, these methods attempted to control pebrine disease by several workers were found to have limited success. Therefore, development of better and more reliable diagnostic methods to detect pebrine during seed production and silkworm rearing has always remained one of the important and valid strategies to eliminate the disease from silkworm crops. Relatively recently recommended delayed mother moth test is a significant step in the area of pebrine disease diagnosis by microscopic test. In this method, the female moths after oviposition are preserved alive at room temperature for a period of 3–4 days before subjecting for microscopic test. This allows improved sporulation of the pathogen facilitating easy and more accurate detection of the disease (Samson, 2000). It has been reported that the rate of multiplication of *N. bombycis* increases substantially with the age of moths and cephalothoracic region had the highest spore concentration, especially around the wing and wing muscles (Sasidharan *et al.*, 1994) and therefore, testing of silk moths 3–4 days after oviposition would be more effective method to detect pebrine with better accuracy. An improved testing method has also been recommended for better detection at egg stage. A sample of egg is incubated at a moderately higher temperature of

32 ± 1°C for 48 hrs to enhance sporulation of *N. bombycis*. Testing of such eggs therefore enhances the chances of detection of the disease. On these lines, even diagnostic techniques based on the principles of immunology were also attempted in several countries including India for detection of pathogen and spore identification, but with only limited success (Baig *et al.*, 1992b).

N. bombycis and closely related spores were diagnosed with antibody-sensitized latex agglutination technique (Hayasaka and Ayuzawa, 1987), slide agglutination technique (Li, 1985; Baig *et al.*, 1992b), the use of ELISA procedures (Kawarabata and Hayasaka, 1987), fluorescent antibody technique (Sato *et al.*, 1981, 1982), serological technique (Grobov and Rodionova, 1985) and SPA co-agglutination technique (Mei and Jin, 1998) etc. Development of monoclonal antibody techniques, which has very high specificity and stability, has played great role in the study of classification and identification of specific microsporidians (Chen *et al.*, 1989; Carlos *et al.*, 1996). Ke *et al.* (1990) raised monoclonal antibodies against *N. bombycis* spores and applied them to identify pebrine and other closely related microsporidian spores infecting silkworms using ELISA procedure. Shi and Jin (1997) reported that agglutination test using N5 McAb (hybridoma cell lines secreting monoclonal antibody) sensitized latex particle is a very practical technique for the diagnosis of pebrine disease. A simple dipstick immunoassay method tried later for diagnosis of pebrine was also unsuccessful in the field. A simple negative staining procedure (Geethabai *et al.*, 1985) and an immunoperoxidase staining procedure (Han and Watanabe, 1987; Kawarabata and Hayasaka,

1987) have been developed for the clarity during examination of spores. Sironmani (1997) has developed a Western blot method to identify the microsporidian infection and observed that immunological reaction with *N. bombycis* infected silkworm larvae and eggs showed the presence of 17-kDa polypeptide, which is specific to infection. He further reported that 17-kDa polypeptide can be used as a virulent marker for the identification of microsporidian infection. DNA based probes have also been developed for identification of *N. bombycis* (Malone and McIvor, 1995).

Several PCR methods based on amplification of rRNA gene fragments are available for the diagnosis and species identification of insect microsporidia (Kawakami *et al.*, 1995, 2001). Molecular techniques developed have more sensitivity and specificity in the detection of the disease (Hatakeyama and Hayasaka, 2001). Nageswararao *et al.*, 2004) have studied the pathogenesis, mode of transmission, tissue specificity of infection and SSU-rRNA gene sequences for the microsporidian isolates from the silkworm, *Bombyx mori*. Genetic characterization and relationship between different microsporidia infecting the mulberry silkworm, using inter simple sequence repeat PCR (ISSR-PCR) analysis have been reported (Nageswararao *et al.*, 2005). They differentiated six different microsporidians through molecular DNA using ISSR-PCR and stated that ISSR-PCR analysis in future may emerge as a powerful tool to detect, diagnose and identify microsporidians, which are difficult to study with microscope because of their extremely small size. A new technique based on identification of intermediary stages has also been suggested for diagnosis of pebrine (Santha *et al.*, 2001).

Immunodiagnostic Assay in Silkworm

Various diagnostic immunoassays have been developed and employed for the detection of silkworm different diseases of the silkworm (Table 3.7).

Though these tests are simple and sensitive, unless standard methods are evolved for their effective field applicability, they cannot create any impact on pebrine disease diagnosis in the field. To maintain the quality of silkworm eggs, several attempts have been made to improve the sampling procedure from time to time (Kurisu, 1986; Kurisu *et al.*, 1985; Fujiwara, 1993). Also, procedures have been developed for detection of pebrine spores in soil/dust, rearing and grainage houses, on mulberry leaves, eggshells/ unhatched eggs, litter etc. (Singh and Saratchandra, 2004). The sample size for examination of faecal matter to detect presence of pebrine has been described by Patil *et al.* (2001). As it is not possible to examine all emerging moths in the commercial grainages, Fujiwara (1993) suggested 20 per cent sampling method and reported probability of detection of the pebrine disease (Table 3.8).

Destruction of disease-causing microorganisms at various levels is general method of preventing and controlling the disease. Surface sterilization of disease free layings, maintenance of strict sanitation, hygienic rearing, frequent and careful examination of stock, disinfections of rearing rooms and appliances, removal of dead and infected larvae to be adopted strictly to get-rid-off the disease. Exposing all the contaminated materials and equipments to direct sunlight, disinfections with 2 per cent formalin solution or 5 per cent bleaching powder solution is the most effective and simple eradication method of the disease.

Table 3.7: List of immunoassays Tested for identification/Detection of Silkworm Pathogens

Sl.No.	*Immunoassay*	*Pathogen*	*References*
1	Precipitin test	*Bm*CPV, *Bm*NPV	Miyajima, 1981.
		*Bm*DNV	Arakawa and Shimizu, 1986.
		*Bm*IFV	Sekijima, 1971.
2	Immunodiffusion test	*Bm*DNV	Arakawa and Shimizu, 1985 &1986; Chen, 1988; Seki, 1986.
		*Bm*IFV	Seki and Sekijima, 1976, Shimizu *et al.*, 1983.
3	Neutralization test	*Bm*CPV	Miyajima, 1981.
		BmIFV	Kurisu *et al.*, 1985.
4	Haemagglutination test	*Bm*CPV	Miyajima and Kawase, 1968.
		BmIFV	Sato and Kawase, 1971.
5	Latex agglutination test	*Bm*CPV	Shimizu and Arakawa, 1986.
		*Bm*DNV	Arakawa and Shimizu, 1986, 1987; Shimizu *et al.*, 1991.
		*Bm*IFV	Shimizu *et al.*, 1983; Sivaprasad *et al.*, 1997.
		*Bm*NPV	Arakawa, 1989; Nataraju *et al.*, 1994 a & b
		N. bombycis	Hayasaka and Ayuzawa, 1987; Baig *et al.*, 1992b; Sengupta, *et al.*, 1990.

Contd...

Table 3.7–Contd...

Sl.No.	*Immunoassay*	*Pathogen*	*References*
6	Fluorescent antibody test	*Bm*DNV	Maeda and Watanabe, 1987.
		*Bm*IFV	Sato *et al*., 1978; Shimizu *et al*., 1983.
		*Bm*NPV	Nagamine *et al*., 1991.
		N. bombycis	Sato *et al*., 1981; Kobayashi and Yamazaki, 1987.
7	Enzyme Linked Immuno Sorbent Assay (ELISA)	*Bm*CPV	Mike *et al*., 1984; Ito *et al*., 1985
		*Bm*DNV	Shi and Ding, 1989; Arakawa and Shimizu, 1987.
		*Bm*IFV	Shimizu, 1982; Sivaprasad *et al*., 2003a.
		*Bm*NPV	Tau *et al*., 1990; Nagamine *et al*., 1991.
		N. bombycis	Kawarabata and Hayasaka, 1987; Miyamoto, 1989; Ke *et al*., 1990.
8	Dipstick Immunoassay	*Bm*NPV	Nataraju *et al*., 1994 a & b
		*Bm*IFV	Nataraju and Datta, 1999; Sivaprasad *et al*., 2003a.

Table 3.8: Probability of Detection of Pebrine in 20 per cent Sampling Method (Index)

No. of Egg Cards (20 layings on each card)	*Population (No. of layings)*	*Pebrine*	*Samples*	*Probability*	
				Non Detectable	*Detectable*
20	400	2	80	0.6400	0.3600
30	600	3	120	0.5120	0.4880
40	800	4	160	0.4096	0.5904
50	1000	5	200	0.3277	0.6723
60	1200	6	240	0.2621	0.7379
80	1600	8	320	0.1678	0.8322
100	2000	10	400	0.1074	0.8926
150	3000	15	600	0.0352	0.9648
200	4000	20	800	0.9885	0.9885
250	5000	25	1000	0.9620	0.9620
300	6000	30	1200	0.9988	0.9988
500	10000	50	2000	1.0000	1.0000

Rate of pebrine infection = 0.5 per cent in female moths

Source: Fuziwara, 1993.

However, the pathogen killing action of the disinfectants is influenced by several factors such as temperature, humidity, concentration of disinfectants and duration of treatment (Kagawa, 1980). Recently, a new disinfectant chlorine dioxide (Serichlor) has been considered as an ideal disinfectant for all the types of rearing/grainage houses. In combination with slaked lime, it is 2.5 times stronger than chlorine and 2 times stronger than sodium-hypochloride. It is least corrosive and non-hazardous. When no single technique is sufficient to check the disease in field, it becomes obligatory to choose a multi-pronged approach.

However, the techniques only help in detecting the disease and the only way out is to destroy the diseased silkworm crops, which causes loss and efforts are to be made at all levels for the prevention of the disease.

A burning problem in the field of microsporidiosis is the increasing number of different microsporidians that are being encountered in silkworm crops (Fuziwara, 1980 and 1993). These microsporidians have shown to exhibit varying degree of virulence and many of them, though infective and pathogenic, have demonstrated low multiplication rate in the silkworm. Some of them have not shown vertical transmission in the host. However, as of today, there has been no specific testing procedure to discriminate these microsporidians in the field to take appropriate action while preparing disease free silkworm seed. If pebrine is to be controlled effectively, a system has to be evolved where either a seed cocoon grower or a seed producer is not put in hardship due to reoccurrence of the disease.

Approaches for Control of Pebrine Disease

- ✩ Produce healthy eggs to avoid embryonic infection. This can be achieved through scientific processing and inspection method of mother moth examination in silkworm egg production center.
- ✩ Dead eggs, dead larvae, dead pupae in the cocoon, dead moths, excrement of larvae from infected trays, exuviae of infected larvae and other possible sources of infection such as contaminated litter should be removed and destroyed.
- ✩ Conduct effective disinfections of grainage rooms, equipments, seed production units and the surroundings.

- Maintain hygienic conditions not only during seed crop rearing but also during egg production.
- Laying should be surface sterilized with 2 per cent formalin for 10 minutes before incubations.
- Inspection of eggshells and sample larvae by standard procedure during each instar for possible presence of pebrine.
- Immediate destruction of infected crops, if noticed pebrine in 1st, 2nd, 3rd and 4th stages of rearing.
- If pebrine is noticed in late final stage (5th stage) or in the cocoon stage, the cocoons are to be sent for reeling.
- If pebrine is noticed after purchase of seed cocoons or in moth stage, the eggs prepared should never be supplied and burnt forthwith.
- Synchronization of rearing to facilitate effective monitoring.
- Monitoring and examination of unequal larvae in the rearing.
- Implementation of seed legislation act in true sense.
- Rearing and grainage operations in same place should be discouraged.
- Practice of hiring appliances should be discouraged.
- Integrated approach is the need of the day for proper disease management in sericulture.
- Destruction of disease causing microsporidians at various levels is the general method of preventing and controlling the disease.

☆ Never pass the silkworm seed which has not been subjected to microscopic examination and has come out disease free in true sense.

Forced Eclosion Test

Sample cocoons from a lot are selected randomly and kept at constant temperature of 33°C to facilitate 1 or 2 days early emergence. The emerged moths are examined and if the lot is noticed infected, are rejected immediately.

Delayed Mother Moth Test

Delayed mother moth test is a significant step in the area of pebrine disease detection by microscopic test. In this method the mother moths after oviposition are collected in groups in perforated cardboard boxes/covers and preserved alive. Alternatively, they can be left on dummy sheets in the oviposition trays itself. The boxes/oviposition trays are properly numbered as per egg sheets and preserved in well-ventilated room at ambient room temperature (25–30°C) for a period of 3–4 days before subjecting for microscopic test. This enhanced sporulation of the pathogen in older moths facilitating easy and more accurate detection of the disease. After stipulated period, moth testing is carried out as per recommended procedure in-vogue. By this method, due to enhanced sporulation in older moths, easy and effective detection of pebrine disease is possible. Even under moderately low infection levels, pebrine can be detected by this method. This technique is very useful during basic seed multiplication and production of P1 seeds. It has been also reported that the rate of multiplication of *N. bombycis* increases substantially with the age of moth and cephalothoraxic region had the highest spore concentration, especially around the wing and wing muscles (Sashidharan *et al.*, 1994) (Table 3.9) and therefore, testing of silk moths 3–4 days after oviposition would be more effective method to detect pebrine with better accuracy.

Table 3.9: Sporulation Rate of *Nosema bombycis* in Different Tissues after Emergence of Moths of Silkworm (After Sashidharan *et al.*, 1994)

Body Parts	*Breeds*	*Quantity of Spores on Different Days After Emergence ($x10^7$/gm wt of tissue)*				
		0 hrs	*24 hrs*	*48 hrs*	*72 hrs*	*96 hrs*
Whole moth	PM	4.39	4.50	5.67	21.90	25.50
	NB18	5.92	6.34	12.40	22.00	28.70
Cephalothorax	PM	8.20	10.50	9.40	35.80	44.00
	NB18	7.10	10.20	14.70	38.40	40.10
Abdomen	PM	1.49	2.60	5.50	14.90	21.60
	NB18	5.02	3.80	7.94	14.00	20.30
Wing	PM	6.30	8.50	11.00	25.00	31.30
	NB18	8.61	12.80	24.45	28.60	34.60
Gut	PM	9.62	10.81	10.60	24.60	22.60
	NB18	8.11	8.94	12.40	20.00	21.20
Fat body	PM	0.19	10.15	0.10	0.20	0.20
	NB18	1.34	2.17	2.10	1.77	2.41

Disposal/Disinfection of Materials used in Testing

Refuse derived from the processes of examination *viz.*, homogenate solution, cotton, muslin cloth etc. should be dumped into a pit after disinfection with 2 per cent bleaching powder solution or dumped and disinfected. Immerse the mixie cups, beakers/tumblers, centrifuge tubes, glass slides, cover-slips, glass rods etc. in 2 per cent bleaching powder solution for 15 minutes followed by washing with detergent. Cover-slips once used should not be re-used. After completing the moth testing, clean the working platform, room floor and adjacent areas by mopping with 2 per cent bleaching powder solution. Maintain strict personnel hygiene.

Preparation of Permanent Slide of Pebrine Spores

- ☆ Make a thin smear on a glass slide and air dry.
- ☆ Fix in methyl alcohol for 2–3 minutes.
- ☆ Air-dry or blots dry the smear.
- ☆ Dilute giemsa stock solution (1 drop giemsa + 1 ml of distilled water) and stain the smear for 45–60 minutes.
- ☆ Wash in distilled water.
- ☆ Air dry or blot dry.
- ☆ Mount in DPX and examine with 600 magnification of microscope.
- ☆ In giemsa stain, pebrine spore appears as pinkish violet or bluish oval body.

Detection of Pebrine Spores in Soil/Dust

- ☆ Collect dust from the rearing house/egg production centers and equipments.
- ☆ Take 5 gm of the soil sample in a beaker and add 20 ml (1:4) of 0.6 per cent Potassium carbonate solution. Stir it thoroughly for 2 minutes. Allow the suspension to settle for 15–20 minutes.
- ☆ Centrifuge the supernatant for 5 minutes at 10,000 r.p.m.
- ☆ Collect the sediment.

- ☆ Take a drop of distilled water on a glass slide and a small quantity of sediment with a glass rod or brush.
- ☆ Add a tiny drop of Indian ink, mount and examine.

Detection of Pebrine Spores on Mulberry Leaves

- ☆ Wash 10–15 mulberry leaves in 100 ml of water.
- ☆ Centrifuge the wash for 8–10 minutes at 10,000 r.p.m.
- ☆ Discard the supernatant.
- ☆ Take a drop of distilled water on a glass slide and small quantity of the sediment with a glass rod or brush.
- ☆ Add a tiny drop of Indian ink, mount and examine.

Detection of Pebrine Spores in Egg-shell/Eggs/Unhatched Eggs

- ☆ Collect head/body pigmented stage eggs/hatched eggshells/unhatched eggs into a porcelain/glass mortar and add 0.6 per cent Potassium carbonate solution and grind thoroughly.
- ☆ After settling, filtering and centrifuging, examine the sediments after dissolving the same.

Detection of Pebrine Spores in Litters

- ☆ Collect 5 gm of litter in a mortar and add 40 ml 0.6 per cent potassium carbonate solution (8 times the weight of litter) and homogenize by grinding. If the resultant homogenate turns out to be viscous, add a few drops of HCI to reduce viscosity.

☆ After settling, filtering and centrifuging dissolve the sediment and observe under microscope.

Adoption of this method in stock race rearing, seed areas and also at silkworm seed rearing to detect spores will help to take up early remedial measures to contain the spread of the disease. The advantages are:

☆ Total elimination of wasteful sacrifice of larvae/ pupae.

☆ Repeated faecal pellet examination may be conducted to ensure detection of infection in the silkworm population without additional cost.

☆ Random sampling method for faecal pellet collection instar-wise (Table 3.10) and centrifugation of homogenate sample enables accurate detection of spores to minimize the incidence of trans-ovarian transmission.

Table 3.10: Faecal Pellet Sample Size for 100 Dfls (After Patil *et al.*, 2001)

Age of Instars		*No. of Trays per Instars (4.5' diameter)*	*Sample Size*	
Instar	*Day*		*No. of samples (10 gm each)*	*Total weight of Faecal Matter (gm)*
I	2	2	1	10
II	2	2	1	10
III	2	4	2	20
IV	2	8	2	20
IV	4	10	3	30
V	2	18	4	40
V	4	25	6	60
V	6	30	8	80

[B] Non-Infectious Diseases

Non-infectious diseases are those which are caused by arthropods, agricultural chemicals and mechanical injuries and that can not be transmitted from infected larvae to healthy larvae.

(*a*) *Poisoning*: Agricultural chemicals, exhaust fumes, coal gas etc.

(*b*) *Physiological Ailments*

(*c*) *Arthropod*: *Acarid* infestation

(*d*) *Strings*: *Euproctis similes, Setora postornata*

(*a*) Poisoning from Agricultural Chemicals

Causal Agent

Organophosphorus, organochlorine, organonitrogen and pesticides of plant origin are the major agricultural chemicals causing poisoning in silkworm if fed with mulberry leaves contaminated with these insecticides.

Symptoms

- ☆ Swinging of anterior half of the body and erratic movement.
- ☆ Enlargement of thoracic region.
- ☆ Vomiting, shortening of body, muscle contraction followed by paralysis and finally death of larvae.

Preventive Measures

- ☆ Avoid feeding of insecticide contaminated mulberry leaf.
- ☆ If insecticides are sprayed in mulberry garden for control of pests and diseases, the safe period recommended for the use of such type of mulberry leaf for feeding to silkworm should strictly be followed.

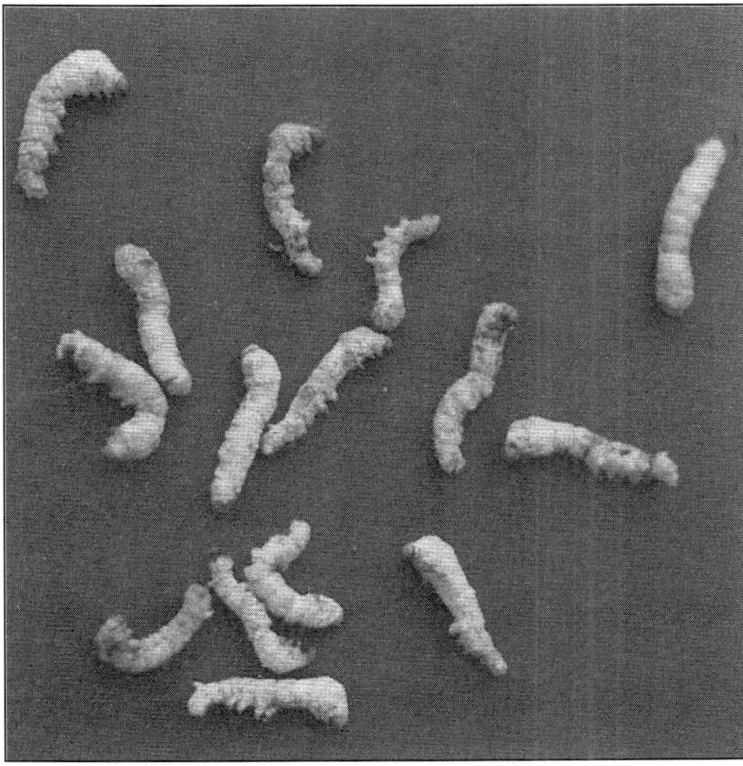

Larvae Affected by Agricultural Chemical Poisoning

☆ All equipments that have come in contact with any of the insecticides should thoroughly be washed with alkaline solution and cleaned properly.

(*b*) Poisoning by Factory Exhaust Fumes

Causal Agent

Silkworms if fed with mulberry leaves contaminated with factory exhaust gases *viz.*, sulphur dioxide, hydrogen fluoride, chlorine etc leads to poisoning in silkworm.

Symptoms

- ☆ Uneven growth.
- ☆ Body atrophies, thorax swells with shrunken posterior part in young larvae.
- ☆ Dark brown lesions near inter-segmental membrane which burst easily and release light yellow fluid in later instars.

Preventive Measures

- ☆ Mulberry fields should at-least be one kilometer away from the factories.
- ☆ If any contamination is noticed, the mulberry leaf should be washed in calcium hydroxide to reduce the degree of poisoning to silkworm. As far as possible such mulberry leaf should not be fed to silkworms.

Chapter 4
Disinfection and Hygiene

The silkworm is affected by a large number of diseases caused by virus, bacteria, fungi and protozoa. These diseases are known to occur in almost all Sericultural regions of the world. The adverse environmental factors like temperature, humidity and poor quality of mulberry leaves reduces the tolerance of the host to the pathogens and hence increases susceptibility to infections. Disinfections and hygiene forms an integral part of healthy and successful silkworm rearing and egg production. Crop losses due to incidence of diseases are one of the major problems encountered by sericulturists in India. The incidence of silkworm diseases and crop losses is greatly influenced by rearing practices, frequency of cropping; conditions of rearing and grainage houses, general hygiene and environmental conditions favourable for pathogen build up and spread. Many pathogens, especially fungal and bacterial spores are light and can be drifted easily by air current, leading to spread of the disease. They have also the ability to remain alive in the environments for longer periods.

Cocoons arriving in the grainages from different sericulture regions of the country can form a continuous source of pathogen entry into seed production units. Processing of batches continuously without providing sufficient time gap, leads to inadequate disinfection and thereby favours pathogen build up in the grainages. Some of the facts about silkworm diseases are:

- ☆ All the infectious diseases of silkworms are caused by pathogens.
- ☆ The adverse environmental factor like temperature, humidity and feeding poor quality of mulberry leaf reduces the tolerance level of host to the pathogens and hence increases susceptibility to infections.
- ☆ The diseases of silkworms are highly contagious and spread very fast.
- ☆ There is no silkworm breed/hybrid, which is completely resistant to all the diseases.
- ☆ The silkworm pathogens survive longer in the rearing and grainage environment and remain infective.
- ☆ The diseases have atypical and typical morphological symptoms.

The disinfection can be defined as an activity, which results in destruction of diseases causing germs. It is the total destruction of diseases caused by pathogens. There are no curative methods for any of the silkworm diseases and hence they can best be prevented rather than cured.

This can be achieved by adoption of proper and effective methods of disinfection before and after every silkworm crop and grainage operations. Therefore, to prevent crop losses due to diseases, disinfection is inevitable. Avoiding the spread of silkworm diseases and production of disease free silkworm seed in the grainage is as much important as checking the spread of diseases in silkworm rearing. Continuous production of seed or rearing without sufficient gap between the two batches does not provide opportunity for regular disinfection and therefore resulting in buildup of pathogens in the rearing and grainage buildings. Silkworm seed is the basic material determining success or failure of a cocoon crop and therefore adopting proper disinfection and hygienic method in preparation of silkworm seed is the foremost step towards raising a healthy silkworm crop.

Since, the species of microorganisms vary and situation in which they may occur differ greatly, no one or two methods are generally applicable. Each situation is a problem in itself and the methods employed depend on the knowledge, ingenuity and purposes of the operator. There are four main reasons for killing, removing or inhibiting microorganisms to maintain hygienic conditions. They are:

- To prevent infection to man, his animals and plants.
- To prevent spoilage of food and other commodities.
- To prevent interference by contaminating microorganisms in various industrial processes that depends on pure culture.

- To prevent contamination of materials used in pure culture work in laboratories (diagnostics, research, industry etc.).

Common methods of killing or removing microorganisms are:

- Destruction by heat (boiler, oven etc), chemical agents (disinfectants), radiation (X-ray, ultraviolet rays etc.), mechanical agents (crushing, shattering by ultrasonic vibration) etc.
- Removal (especially bacteria) by filtration, high seed centrifugation etc.
- Inhibition by low temperatures (refrigeration, dry ice), desiccation (drying process), high osmotic pressures (lymph, brines etc), chemicals and drugs etc.

Selection of Disinfectants

Several disinfectants are available in the market but only few are widely used. The disinfectants available in the market can be grouped as:

- Halogens (Chlorine, Iodine etc.).
- Heavy metals ($HgCl_2$, Mercurochrome, Metaphen, Protargol, etc.).
- Phenol compounds (Lysol, Creosols etc.).
- Alcohols (Ethyl and Isopropyl).
- Formaldehydes (strong reducing agent which inactivates even enzymes).
- Ethylene oxide (Carboxide, Cryocide etc.).

Qualities of an Ideal Disinfectant

Ideal disinfectant is selected taking into consideration of various factors. The ideal disinfectant must possess the following qualities:

- ☆ Highly effective against a wide variety of micro-organisms in concentration as low as to be economical for use as well as harmless to human beings, domestic animals and non-toxic to plants.
- ☆ Non-injurious and non-staining to materials like fabrics, furniture or metal wares and non-offensive to odour or taste.
- ☆ As specific as possible for microorganisms.
- ☆ Does not damage the building, materials, appliances and equipments.
- ☆ A good surface tension reducer (have good wetting and penetrating properties).
- ☆ Stable in storage.
- ☆ Readily available in market and less expensive.
- ☆ Easily applied under household or other practical conditions of use.
- ☆ Completely microbicidal within a few minutes or an hour at the most and not inducing macrobiotics, leading to a false sense of security.
- ☆ Non-corrosive.

But, no single disinfectants have all these ideal properties. Some agents may be ideal under some conditions but not under others, *e.g.*, Cresol may be ideal for floors or sanitary purposes but harmful to infants.

Conditions Necessary for Effective Disinfections

It is established that disinfectants respond better under some specific conditions whereby disinfection becomes perfect and effective, such as:

Hydration

Considerable quantity of water is required to facilitate the action of disinfectants, *e.g.*, dehydrated protein to coagulate is difficult since it will turn brown or char. Moreover, resistance of bacterial endospore to heat is probably caused in part by their extremely dehydrated conditions.

Time

No disinfectant, as ordinarily used, acts instantly. Sufficient time for contact must be allowed for whatever chemical and physical reactions to occur. The time required will depend on the nature of the disinfectant, concentration, pH and temperature, nature of target organism and existence of the bacterial population of cells having varying susceptibilities to the disinfectant.

Temperature

With respect to the microbicidal action of heat, temperature is inversely related to time. In case of chemical microbicides, as a rule, the warmer the disinfectant, the more effective is its action. Higher temperatures generally reduce the surface tension, increase acidity, decrease viscosity and diminish adsorption.

Concentration

Effectiveness of a disinfectant is generally related to concentration exponentially, but not linearly. For example, doubling a 0.5 per cent concentration of phenol in aqueous solution does not merely double the killing rate. Doubling the concentration again may increase the effect by only a negligible amount. There is clearly an optimum concentration of phenol at about 1 per cent. Thus, a concentration of a disinfectant beyond a certain point accomplishes increasingly less and is wasteful.

pH

An important factor in detergency is pH which is a measure of acidity or alkalinity. As the pH of the solution increases *i.e* becomes more alkaline, the efficiency of the product increases. There are limits to this, as too high pH will frequently result in deleterious effects on the surface being cleaned or disinfected. In general, a pH not higher than 10.5 is recommended. As a general rule, the lethal or toxic action of harmful agents involving physical and chemical actions is increased by increased concentration of 'H' or 'OH'–ions.

Osmotic Pressure

Fluids of high osmotic pressure (*e.g.* food preserving syrups and brines) tend to dehydrate the cell contents and so increase resistance of microbial cells to heat and chemical disinfectants.

Surface Tension

Surface tension is of basic importance in disinfection. There are two aspects of this factor, adsorption of surface disinfectants or interfering substances on the surface of the cells and the effect of disinfectants on the wetting and spreading properties of the solution. Both affect contact between disinfectants and microorganisms.

Materials Required for Disinfections

Disinfectants, detergent, sprayer, buckets, measuring jars, weighing scale (balance), gas masks, slaked lime, hand gloves and muslin cloths are required during disinfection.

Method of Disinfections: Disinfection methods are classified broadly of two types; physical and chemical.

A] Physical Methods (Burning, burying and exposure to sunlight)

The physical method includes the use of physical agents such as ultraviolet radiation, flame, dry heat and streams etc. In sericulture, exposing the grainage or rearing equipments to bright sunlight for 8–10 hrs is a very economical method of disinfection under Indian conditions. Heat is the major destroyer. Dry heat destroys the microorganism by oxidation and is non-corrosive. Dry heat requires longer exposure time and or higher temperature. Use of boiling water is another effective method of disinfection. In this method maximum temperature of 100°C can be obtained and exposure of 10–30 minutes is found effective. Moreover, it is cumbersome and somewhat non-reliable method. However, best results can be achieved by a combination of both physical and chemical methods.

B] Chemical Methods

Chemical means of disinfection involves only those chemicals which have germicidal activity against targeted microbes. The use of chemical for disinfection achieved momentum since 1867, when Lister stated that phenol (carbolic acid) would kill microorganism. From then onwards, various chemicals have been tested for their germicidal activities and few of them are found effective in sericulture also.

Formalin

It is the most commonly used disinfectants in all sericultural countries. Formalin is aqueous solution of formaldehyde. It is commercially available in the form of 36–40 per cent formaldehyde. The specific gravity is 1.081 in 36 per cent and 1.087 in 40 per cent formalin. The molecular formula of formalin is CH_2O. The disinfecting action of formalin is due to the reducing process of formaldehyde *i.e* HCOH + O = HCOOH. Formaldehyde takes oxygen out of the germ cells leading to death of the germs. A mixture of 2 per cent formalin + 0.5 per cent staked lime is very effective solution that can be used for disinfection purpose. Formaldehyde upon storage polymerizes into trioxymetylene, which is ineffective as spray and therefore storage of formaldehyde for long time is not advisable. The action of formalin takes place under wet conditions and therefore, the surface of equipments and walls should be drenched with the solution. The action of formalin is faster and more pronounced at temperature above 25°C and humidity > 70 per cent. The action is greatly reduced at temperature below 20°C. This mixture is more effective only if grainage and rearing houses/rooms/ buildings could be closed to near airtight conditions. In India, more than 90 per cent of the rearing and grainage buildings are not suitable for disinfection with formalin as they are open type dwelling houses. However, formalin is also reported to be a carcinogen and therefore use of it as far as possible should be avoided.

Bleaching Powder

Bleaching powder is also called chlorinated lime. It is white amorphous powder with a characteristic of pungent odour of chlorine. The efficacy of bleaching powder is very much dependent on the level of active chlorine in the compound. For effective disinfection, a high-grade bleaching powder with active chlorine content of 30 per cent and above must be used. Bleaching powder when comes in contact with water produces weak acid (HCl) and releases nascent oxygen which has strong oxidizing action against germ cells. It should be stored in sealed bags, away from moisture and light to avoid degradation which rendered it ineffective. Freshly prepared solution of bleaching powder gives the best results. A 2 per cent bleaching powder in 0.3 per cent slaked lime is used for disinfection as spray. The action of bleaching powder is optimal under wet conditions and therefore, surface of appliances, equipments, walls of grainage and rearing rooms should be drenched properly with this solution.

Slaked Lime (Calcium hydroxide)

It is very widely used bed disinfectant and drying agent in sericulture. It absorbs moisture and can be used to regulate bed humidity and maintain hygiene in rearing and grainage buildings. It has strong antiviral action. Application of lime dust alone or in combination with bleaching powder in and around rearing and grainage houses and premises improves hygiene in the environment. It is prepared from burnt lime stone or shells by sprinkling water followed by pulverizing and sieving. Lime stone or $CaCO_3$ is burnt to produce quick lime (CaO) which when hydrated forms slaked lime (Calcium hydroxide) [$Ca(OH)_2$] which is used as disinfectant in sericulture.

Paraformaldehyde

It is white crystalline substance with a strong odour of

formalin formed by polymerization of formaldehyde. It is effective for fumigation purpose and is an ingredient of certain bed disinfectants. On heating, it sublimates and releases formaldehyde gas which inactivates the pathogens in wet condition and therefore the humidity of the room should be simultaneously increased to maintain the optimum level of requirement for grainage and rearing.

Chlorine Dioxide

Chlorine dioxide (ClO_2) is marketed in different names such as sanitech, serichlor etc. It is an ideal disinfectant suitable for all types of rearing and grainage buildings. In combination with slaked lime, it is effective against all silkworm pathogens. It is a strong oxidizing agent, 2.5 times stronger than chlorine and two times stronger than sodium hypo-chloride. The disinfectant available at 20,000 ppm concentration is strong oxidizing agent. It is effective at broader ranges of pH and less reactive with organic compounds. It is least corrosive and non-hazardous. Chlorine dioxide (Sanitech) 500 ppm in 0.5 per cent slaked lime may be used for disinfection. It is stable at room temperature and may be activated at the time of its use. It possesses tolerable odor and least corrosive at recommended concentration of use.

Quantity Requirement of Disinfectants

Quantity requirement of disinfectant is estimated based on the surface area of the rearing/grainage building or trays and appliances to be disinfected. The quantity requirement may be estimated as:

(*a*) *Room*: (Total area in square meter)

Area of roof and floor : L x B x 2

	Area of two opposite walls	: L x B x 2
	Area of two other side walls	: L x B x 2
(*b*)	Trays (wooden/plastic)	: L x B x 2 x Number of trays
(*c*)	Bamboo trays	: $\Pi r^2 x$ 2 x Number of trays

The disinfectant solution should be prepared @ one liter per 2.5 square meters of area to be disinfected.

Solution required in liters =

$$\frac{\text{Total area in square meters}}{2.5}$$

Preparation of Disinfectant Solutions

Disinfectant solution should be prepared a fresh before every use.

(*i*) 2 per cent Formalin Solution

Commercial formalin contains 36 per cent formaldehyde. This is diluted to prepare 2 per cent solution of formalin as follows:

$$\frac{\text{Concentration of available formalin} - \text{Concentration of formalin required}}{\text{Concentration of required formalin}} = \text{Parts of water to be added in one part of formalin}$$

$$i.e \ \frac{36-2}{2} = 17 \text{ parts of water}$$

$$\text{or } N1V1 = N2V2 \text{ or } V1 = \frac{N2V2}{N1} \text{ } i.e \text{ } V1 = \frac{2x100 \text{ (ml)}}{36} = 5.55$$

$$100.00 - 5.55 = 94.45 \text{ ml water;}$$

$$\text{Ratio} = 94.45{:}\ 5.55 = 17{:}\ 1$$

where,

N1: Given strength of solution

N2: Desired strength of solution

V1: Volume of stock chemical required

V2: Desired volume of solution to be prepared

Practically, for all disinfection purposes, one part of formalin can be mixed with 17 parts of water to prepare 2 per cent formalin solution (Table 4.1) from commercially available formalin (36 per cent).

Table 4.1: Preparation of 2 per cent Formalin Solution of Different Quantities From Commercially Available 36 per cent Stock Solution of Formalin

Sl.No.	*Total Volume of Solution Required (liter)*	*Quantity of Formalin Required*	*Water to be Added (liter)*	*Ratio of Formalin : Water*
1.	1.00	56 ml	0.944	1 : 17
2.	5.00	280 ml	4.720	1 : 17
3.	10.00	560 ml	9.440	1 : 17
4.	15.00	840 ml	14.160	1 : 17
5.	20.00	1.120 liter	18.880	1 : 17
6.	25.00	1.400 liter	23.600	1 : 17
7.	30.00	1.680 liter	28.320	1 : 17
8.	35.00	1.960 liter	33.040	1 : 17
9.	50.00	2.800 liter	47.200	1 : 17
10.	75.00	4.200 liter	70.800	1 : 17
11.	100.00	5.600 liter	94.400	1 : 17

If commercial formalin contains 36 formaldehyde, ratio of formalin and water in preparation of solution of different concentration of formalin will be as follows (Table 4.2).

Table 4.2: Preparation of Different Concentrations of Formalin

Sl.No.	*Concentration of Formalin Required (per cent)*	*Concentration of Available Formalin (per cent)*	*Ratio of Water : Formalin*
1.	1	36	35.00 : 1
2.	2	36	17.00 : 1
3.	3	36	11.00 : 1
4.	4	36	8.00 : 1
5.	5	36	6.20 : 1
6.	6	36	5.00 : 1
7.	7	36	4.10 : 1
8.	8	36	3.50 : 1
9.	9	36	3.00 : 1
10.	10	36	2.60 : 1

(*ii*) Formalin 2 per cent + 0.5 per cent Slaked Lime Mixture

After preparation of 2 per cent formalin solution, slaked lime is added to it @ 5 gm in one liter of formalin solution. Slaked lime is prepared by sprinkling water on burnt limestone and pulverizes it into fine powder of 200–250 mesh size.

Estimation of Quantity of Disinfectant Required

The quantity required for disinfection may be calculated adopting the following procedure (example)"

Length of floor (L) = 20'

Breadth of floor (B) = 15'

Floor area for disinfection = L x B =

20' x 15' = 300 square feet or 28 m^2

The disinfectant required for disinfection of rearing/ grainage house is @ 2 liter/square meter floor area or 185 ml/sq. feet floor area. Therefore, disinfection solution required = Total area x @ 2 liter/sq. meter or 28 m^2 x 2 = 56 liter.

Disinfection for outside the rearing/grainage house and appliances is to be added in this quantity. Additional disinfectant required for appliances is estimated to be 25 per cent of the solution required for floor area *i.e* 56 x 25 per cent = 14 liters.

Additional disinfectant required for outside the rearing/ grainage house is estimated to be 10 per cent of the solution required for floor area *i.e* 56 x 10 per cent = 5.6 liters. Hence, total quantity of disinfectant required = 56 + 14 + 5.6 = 75.6 or 75 liters (Table 4.1).

(*iii*) 5 per cent Bleaching Powder Solution (Stable 30 per cent chlorine)

Solution of 5 per cent bleaching powder is prepared by dissolving 50 gm of the chemical in one liter of water (ratio; 1: 20). The mixture is agitated well. It is filtered through a layer of muslin cloth and the clear solution is used for spraying/disinfection. A ready reckonor for preparation of 5 per cent bleaching powder solution of different volumes is presented in Table 4.3.

The ratio of powder and water to be mixed for preparation of different concentrations of bleaching powder solution is presented in Table 4.4.

Table 4.3: Preparation of Different Quantities of 5 per cent Bleaching Powder Solution

Sl.No.	Total Volume of Solution Required (liter)	Bleaching Powder Required (gm)	Water to be Added (liter)	Ratio of Bleaching Powder : Water
1.	1.00	50	1.00	1: 20
2.	5.00	250	5.00	1: 20
3	10.00	500	10.00	1: 20
4.	15.00	750	15.00	1: 20
5.	20.00	1000	20.00	1: 20
6.	25.00	1250	25.00	1: 20
7.	30.00	1500	30.00	1: 20
8.	35.00	1750	35.00	1: 20
9.	50.00	2500	50.00	1: 20
10.	100.00	5000	100.00	1: 20

Table 4.4: Requirement of Bleaching Powder for Preparation of Different Concentration of Solution

Sl.No.	Concentration of Solution Required (per cent)	Quantity of Water (liter)	Quantity of Powder (gm)	Ratio of Bleaching Powder : Formalin
1.	1.00	1.00	10.00	1: 10
2	2.00	1.00	20.00	1: 50
3.	3.00	1.00	30.00	1: 33
4.	4.00	1.00	40.00	1:25
5.	5.00	1.00	50.00	1:20
6.	6.00	1.00	60.00	1:17
7.	7.00	1.00	70.00	1: 14
8.	8.00	1.00	80.00	1: 13
9.	9.00	1.00	90.00	1: 11
10.	10.00	1.00	100.00	1: 10

$$\text{Quantity of chemical required} = \frac{\text{Per cent of solution to be prepared} \times \text{Quantity of solution required}}{100}$$

Example

(*a*) 2% of 1 liter solution $= \dfrac{2\% \times 1000 \text{ (ml)}}{100} = 20$ gm

(*b*) 5% of 1 liter solution $= \dfrac{5\% \times 1000 \text{ (ml)}}{100} = 50$ gm

(*c*) 2% of 75 liter solution $= \dfrac{2\text{x } 75{,}000 \text{ ml}}{100} =$ 1500 gm or 1.5 kg.

(*iv*) Bleaching Powder–Slaked Lime Mixture

High-grade bleaching powder is mixed with finely powdered 200–250 mesh size slaked lime @ 50 gm per 950 gm of lime (1:19) to prepare 5 per cent bleaching powder solution. The mixture is used for dusting at the entrance and rearing and grainage building surroundings to maintain proper hygiene.

(*v*) Slaked Lime Powder

Burnt rock lime (limestone) or shell lime is procured, water is sprinkled and it is allowed to become powder. This is further pulverized, sieved and made into the form of fine powder, which can be readily used. Application of lime dust in and around rearing and grainage building and premises improves hygiene in the environment.

(*vi*) Chlorine Dioxide (Sanitech 20,000 ppm stable)

It is powerful, users' friendly, non-hazardous, safe and effective disinfectant for silkworm rearing and grainage house and equipments. Unlike formalin, it is non-carcinogenic. It is capable of successfully destroying microbial and all silkworm pathogens. Sanitech is 2.5 times more potent than chlorine and 50 times more effective than any hypochlorite like bleaching powder. Demands no airtight conditions of rearing and grainages houses for its action. There is no limitation of temperature and humidity for its action. Sanitech do not have corroding action on metallic items and rearing equipments at the recommended concentration. It remains in association with water as oxygen does in water. Sanitech is effective on a broad pH range (pH: 5–9). It does not give pungent smell or suffocation. Chlorine dioxide (500 ppm) in 0.5 per cent slaked lime can be prepared as:

Solution A

Add 50 gm of activator crystal to 500 ml Sanitech (ClO_2) solution in a clean basin/bucket to activate chlorine dioxide, stir and allow 10 minutes for complete dissolution of crystals. Colour changes to light yellow. Add the prepared 500 ml yellow solution to 19 liters of water to get 19.5 liter of solution.

Solution B

Dissolve 100 gm of slaked lime powder in 500 ml water in another clean container and allow for some time to settle down.

Mix solution 'A' and 'B' to obtain a total of 20 liters of disinfectants. One liter of Sanitech makes 40 liters of disinfectants. For disinfection of one square meter of area, two liter of Sanitech solution is required. To prepare 2.5 per cent Chlorine Dioxide + 0.5 per cent slaked lime solution of different quantities, the requirement will be as detailed in Table 4.5.

Table 4.5: Preparation of 2.5 per cent Chlorine Dioxide + 0.5 per cent Slaked Lime Solution

Sl.No.	*Volume of Solution Required (liter)*	*Quantity of Sanitech Required (liter)*	*Water to be Added (liter)*	*Activator Crystal Required (gm)*	*Quantity of Lime to be Added (gm)*
1.	5.00	0.125	4.875	12.50	25.00
2.	10.00	0.250	9.750	25.00	50.00
3.	20.00	0.500	19.500	50.00	100.00
4.	30.00	0.750	29.250	75.00	150.00
5.	40.00	1.000	39.000	100.00	200.00
6.	50.00	1.250	48.750	125.00	250.00
7.	60.00	1.500	58.500	150.00	300.00
8.	80.00	2.000	78.000	200.00	400.00
9.	100.00	2.500	97.500	250.00	500.00

Disinfection of Rearing and Grainage Houses, Appliances etc.

Drench all parts of rearing and grainage building inside and outside and appliances uniformly using gutter or jet sprayer with required quantity of disinfectant (@ 2.0 liter/ m^2 floor area of rearing/grainage house + 25 per cent of disinfectant solution for appliances + 10 per cent for outside of the building). After disinfection, rearing or grainage houses must be closed for a minimum period of 24 hrs. Rearing trays, cocoon storage trays, oviposition trays etc. should not be smeared with cow dung. Disinfected rearing or grainage houses must be opened at least 24 hrs before the use for rearing and grainage operation.

Dipping the Appliances in Disinfectant

Disinfect the rearing or grainage appliances in 2 per cent bleaching powder in 0.3 per cent slaked lime solution by dipping for at least 10 minutes in disinfection tank. The disinfection tank of 2 feet depth and 4 feet diameter is considered suitable for disinfection purpose. Prepare the disinfectant solution of required quantity and concentration and fill half of the tank. To determine the volume of the tank and the disinfectant solution to be prepared the formula llr^2h is used.

Example

The volume of tank of 4 feet diameter and 2 feet height

Diameter = 4 feet and therefore radius (r) = 4 ÷ 2 = 2; as only half of the tank is to be filled, the height of solution in the tank will be 2 ÷ 2 = 1'

Therefore, llr^2h = 3.14 x 2 x 2 x 1 = 12.56 cubic feet

One cubic feet holds 28 liters of solution, therefore 12.56 cubic feet will hold

12.56 x 28 = 352 liters of solution.

To prepare 352 liters of 2 per cent bleaching powder in 0.3 per cent slaked lime solution, the requirement will be as follows -

Requirement of water = 352 liters

Requirement of bleaching powder = 352 x 20 gm = 7.040 kg.

Requirement of 0.3 per cent slaked lime = 352 x 3 gm = 1.056 kg.

Prepare 352 liters of solution and fill in the disinfection tank. Dip the appliances as many as possible to submerge in the solution. After 10 minutes the appliances are removed from the disinfection tank and carried directly to the disinfected rearing or grainage houses. Afterwards, another set of appliances is dipped in the solution. This system will continue for 8–10 times. The solution is discarded after using 10 times and fresh solution is prepared for the purpose.

Maintenance of hygienic conditions is ensured by rigorous practice of disinfection on the vulnerable foci of infection. Disinfection of rearing and grainage rooms and appliances to prevent vertical transmission of pathogens is very much essential which is to be carried out before rearing and grainage operation with available disinfectants to destroy pathogens. Disinfection of other sources of contamination/infection to prevent horizontal transmission of pathogens is:

- ☆ Surface sterilization of silkworm eggs.
- ☆ Disinfection of rearing and grainage rooms/ building.
- ☆ Disinfection of surrounding areas of rearing and grainage building.
- ☆ Disinfection of rearing and grainage appliances, oviposition and storage room.
- ☆ Personal hygiene.

Before to use the disinfectants, it is of utmost importance to think about the residual effect of the disinfectants towards environmental pollution and positive side effects on the persons who are handling the disinfectants as also their pets. As no disinfectant is absolutely free from the above, only those disinfectants are to be selected where the side effects are minimal. At present Chlorine dioxide ranks first being the most eco-friendly and users friendly disinfectant available to the sericulture industry. Regular practice of disinfection in all possible ways has proved to be very much effective to maintain hygiene and its successful implementation will minimize crop loss due to diseases.

Schedule of disinfection and details of activity to be carried out during disinfections of rearing house is presented below (Table 4.6)

Table 4.6: Schedule of Disinfection

Day	*Activity*	*Details of Activity*
After the completion of previous crops	1	Collection and burning of diseased larvae, melted and flimsy cocoons etc.
	2	Flaming the floss of mountages and disinfection by fumigation (formalin 10 per cent) or by flame gun
	3	1st disinfection of rearing house and appliances with bleaching powder 2 per cent in 0.3 per cent slaked lime or Sanitech 2.5 per cent in slaked lime 0.5 per cent)
5 days before brushing	4	Cleaning and washing
	5	Sun drying of appliances
4 days before brushing	6	Optimal disinfection of rearing house with 0.3 per cent slaked lime
3 days before brushing	7	2nd disinfection of rearing house and appliances with bleaching powder 2 per cent in 0.3 per cent slaked lime or Sanitech 2.5 per cent in slaked lime 0.5 per cent)
2 days before brushing	8	Dusting disinfectant (5 per cent bleaching powder in slaked lime) in front of rearing house and to the passage.
	9	Open the windows of rearing house for ventilation of rearing house
1 day before brushing	10	Preparation for brushing

Source: Nataraju *et al*., 2005.

Maintenance of Hygiene during Rearing, Grainage and Egg Production

- ☆ Do not use rearing and grainage appliances without disinfection.
- ☆ Avoid overlapping rearing or grainage operations.
- ☆ Do not borrow appliances for use.
- ☆ Brushing of new crops before the completion of previous crops should be avoided.
- ☆ The compost pit should be away from the rearing house.
- ☆ Mulberry leaves should be stored in separate room.
- ☆ Bed disinfectant should be dusted as per recommendation.
- ☆ Avoid injury to silkworm larvae during bed cleaning, rearing, transferring and mounting.
- ☆ Diseased and non-spinning larvae are to be picked with chopstick and dispose them off in 2 per cent bleaching powder in 0.3 per cent slaked lime solution in a basin. Do not throw them on the floor of the rearing house.
- ☆ Seed cocoons should be spread over sheet papers in trays which are disinfected to avoid contamination.
- ☆ Melted and dead cocoons should be separated from a batch and subjected for microscopical examination.
- ☆ Hand gloves, aprons and foot-wears should be used while handling seed cocoons, pupae and moths etc. in the grainages and larvae in the rearing houses.

- Maintain personal hygiene throughout rearing and grainage operations.
- Restrict the entry of persons in the rearing or grainage buildings.
- Disinfect the silkworm eggs with 2 per cent formalin for 5–10 minutes and wash with clean water, dry them in shade. Disinfect also before initiation of incubation.
- Moth/larval testing area should be properly disinfected every day before and after carrying out the microscopical examination.
- At the passage of entrance to rearing and grainage building, sprinkle 5 per cent bleaching powder in slaked lime @ 18 gm/sq.ft.
- Rearers or grainures or any other person involved in rearing or grainage operation entering to the rearing or grainage rooms must disinfect foot and hand before entry. Hand should be thoroughly washed with alkaline germicidal soap.
- The foot mat at the entrance of building is to be soaked in 2 per cent bleaching powder in 0.3 per cent slaked lime solution. The foot mat must be soaked in disinfectant solution daily.
- Separate footwear and clean apron should be used.
- Wipe the floor daily with 2 per cent bleaching powder in 0.3 per cent slaked lime solution. If the floor is of mud, dust 5 per cent bleaching powder in slaked lime at an interval of 3–4 days without fail.
- Larval or moth testing equipments such as crushing sets, mixie cups, glass rods, beakers, funnels etc.

Table 4.7: Disinfectants and their Requirement for 200 sq. ft. Floor Area of Rearing or Grainage Building

Item to Disinfectant	*Mode of Disinfection*	*Quantity Required*	*Quantity of Disinfectants Required*		
			Bleaching Powder (kg)	*Slaked Lime (kg)*	*Detergent (kg)*
Rearing or Grainage house (200 sq. ft. or 18.58 sq. mtr) and appliances (8 stands and 160 trays).	Spray disinfection, cleaning and washing with 2% bleaching powder in 0.3% slaked lime + 50% for appliances.	Floor area of grainage/rearing house x 2 liters/ sq. mtr + 50% for appliances *i.e* 18.58 x 2 = 37.00 + 18.50 liters = 55.5 liters.	1.11	0.166	–
Disinfection of appliances by soaking the trays, plastic sheets etc.	2% bleaching powder in 0.3% slaked lime solution.	500 liters.	10.00	1.500	–
Spray disinfection of grainage/rearing house and surroundings.	0.3% slaked lime solution + 25% for surroundings	37 liters + 9.25 liters =46.25 liters.	–	0.138	–
Spray disinfection of grainage/rearing house and appliances.	2% formalin + 0.5% detergent + 50% for appliances + 25% for rearing/grainage house and surroundings	37 liters +18.5 liters + 9.25 liters = 64.75 liters or 65.00 liters.	–	–	0.325

should be cleaned and disinfected after every sample.

- ✰ The rearing or grainage waste like diseased/crushed larvae/moths, melted cocoons, sheet papers etc. should be treated with 2 per cent bleaching powder solution and deposited in a disinfection pit (soak pit) which must be away from the rearing/grainage building.
- ✰ Cocoons should not be stored nearby the seed processing area and separate store room should be provided for them.
- ✰ The grainage/rearing staff should properly be trained in different procedures of disinfections and maintenance of hygiene.

Chapter 5

Forewarning and Forecasting of Pests and Diseases

(I) PEST SURVEILLANCE AND FORECASTING

(A) Pest Surveillance

Pest surveillance is defined as 'periodical assessment of pests' populations and their damage' or 'watch kept on a pest for the purpose of decision making in pest management'. Pest surveillance can provide the necessary information to determine the feasibility of a pest control programme. Method of sampling, surveillance and forecasting of insect population for integrated pest management in sericulture is described by Singh *et al.* (2004). Pest surveillance comprises of three basic components:

- ☆ Determination of the level of incidence of pest species.

- ☆ Determination of what loss the incidence will cause.
- ☆ Determination of economic benefits the control will provide.

(*i*) Objectives of Pest Surveillance

- ☆ To monitor the presence of a pest and
- ☆ To determine the population density, dispersion, damage caused etc.

(*ii*) Survey

Regular survey activity is necessary for successful surveillance programmes. An insect pest, survey is 'a detailed collection of insect population information at a particular time in a given area'. These surveys are both qualitative and quantitative. The qualitative surveys aim at the pest detection, employed with newly introduced pests and often precedes quantitative survey. The quantitative surveys attempt to define numerically the abundance of an insect population in time and space. It is useful to predict future population trends and to assess damage potentials.

(*iii*) Sampling

It is 'a representative part of the total population and base our estimate on that part'.

(*iv*) Sampling Techniques

Surveillance requires suitable sampling techniques. A sampling technique is 'the method used to collect information for a single sample'. The sampling techniques include direct counts (*in-situ* counts); knock down, netting, trapping (use of light trap, pheromone trap and sticky trap), extraction from soil etc.

(*v*) Sampling Programme

It is 'the procedure for employing the sampling techniques in time and space'. Sampling programme describes when sampling is to begin, location of samples, number of samples and how often samples should be collected.

(*vi*) Decision Making

Decision making is the keystone in insect pest management programmes. It indicates the course of action to be taken in any pest management. Identification of pests, biology and behaviour of the pests, natural regulating factors, need for control measures, timing of control measures and selection of suitable control measures are critical factors in decision-making.

(*vii*) Indices in Pest Surveillance

(*a*) Economic Damage

It is 'the amount of injury, which justifies the cost of artificial control measures'.

(*b*) Economic Thresh-hold (ET) and Economic Injury Level (EIL)

Economic threshold is defined as the average population density of a pest over a unit area where control measures are to be taken up in order to prevent an increasing pest population from reaching economic injury level. Economic damage is considered as the amount of energy, which will justify the cost of control measures. In simple term, the economic threshold is 'the level at which management action should be taken to prevent population reaching EIL'. It is to be kept in mind that the added cost of pest management must be less than or equal to the added benefits to justify its use otherwise implementation of control measures would lead to significant waste to farmers.

Factors Affecting the ETL

- ☆ Crop value/market value
- ☆ Management costs
- ☆ Degree of injury
- ☆ Crop susceptibility to injury

The relationship between ETL and market value is inverse. The crop market value is always under fluctuations. Management costs tend to be more stable than crop market value. The degree of injury by various type of feeding is also important. The relationship between injury and the crop yield is the most important factor of the ETL.

$$\text{Gain thresh-hold} = \frac{\text{Management cost (Rs./unit)}}{\text{Market value (Rs./kg)/unit}} = \text{kg/unit}$$

$$\text{EIL} = \frac{\text{Gain thresh-hold}}{\text{Loss per insect}}$$

Assessment of Silkworm Crop Loss due to Pest Incidence

Replicated field trials are generally used to assess silkworm crop losses due to pest attack with randomized blocks where some blocks are kept free from pest attack through adoption of pest control measures whereas other blocks are allowed to be damaged by naturally occurring populations of pests. The experiments are repeated and extensive data are collected on pest incidence and cocoon yield loss. The obtained data is computed as suggested by Nataraju *et al.*, (2005) as furnished below:

Let, AY = Actual cocoon yield/100 Dfls

x = mean cocoon yield in un-infested crop

y = mean cocoon yield in infested crop

p = Per cent larvae infested

Then Z = Co-efficient of loss which can be calculated as:

$$Z = (x - y)\ 100/x$$

The Per cent economic loss (EL) = Zp/100

And the expected yield 'Y' in the absence of pest infestation is:

$$Y = 100\ (AY)/100 - EL$$

The Economic loss = Y– AY

Production analysis is used to determine yield losses. Each regression co-efficient is multiplied by the average value of the particular yield limiting factor. This provides an estimate of the overall impact of this factor on sampled yield.

(B) Forecasting

It is 'an advance knowledge of probable pest infestations (out breaks) in a crop for planning the cropping pattern in such a way as to minimize the damage but also to get the best advantage of the pest control measures' or 'forewarning of the forthcoming infestations of pests'.

Forecasts are being done based on populations studies, studies on the pest's life history and field studies of the effect of climatic factors on the pest and its environment. Forecasting service serves:

(*i*) To predict the forthcoming infestation level of the pest. This is essential in justifying the use of control measures.

(*ii*) To find out the critical stage at which the applications of insecticides would afford maximum protection. The forecasts may be of two types *viz.*:

(*a*) *Short-term Forecasting*: It covers a particular season or two successive seasons and it is based on simple sampling.

(*b*) *Long-term Forecasting*: It covers large areas and it is based on possible effects of weather on the insect abundance or by extrapolating from the present population density into the future.

The distribution of pests and the extent of damage caused by them are directly related to the frequency of incidence. Hence, forecasting extent of incidence, damage and range of pest population has to be taken into account. In fact, this type of forecast raises two standards *i.e* standard for quantum of incidence and standard for forecasting incidence durations. Shorter the forecasting period higher is the accuracy. Contrarily, with increase in other influential factors, accuracy suffers. Currently, systematic scientific data are lacking for assessment (forecast) reports on silkworm pests. Also the forecasts for the time of pest incidence are not as perfect as those of food grains, cotton and other crops. There is an urgent need for proper data accumulation to improve the accuracy of assessment of impact of pest. The principle aim of pest forecasting is to ensure that control measures, notably the use of chemical pesticides, are adopted only when needed to prevent economic damage and at the correct time for maximum effectiveness. This would help to ensure that chemicals are used to supplement 'natural controls', as well as minimizing the problems created by overuse and misuse of pesticides. Forecasting is therefore, fundamental to many Integrated Pest Management (IPM) programmes. Three major components involved in developing and implementing the forecasting scheme are:

- Defining the economic threshold for pest attack;
- Developing relevant monitoring and forecasting procedures;
- Providing a means for implementing the forecasting programme within the crop production system.

The first consideration is to assess whether a practical forecast is feasible, given the nature of the particular pest problem, the objectives of the grower and the control options available. Much will depend upon whether early levels of pest incidence can be related to future levels of damage on the crop.

Volume of Pesticide required per Unit Area

In a pesticide application programme, it is very essential to know the volume of spraying or dusting material required for an effective coverage of an area. If the volume of liquid to be sprayed is taken more, the pesticide will be wasted and the effective concentration will be less. On the other hand, if the volume of the liquid taken is less, it may not cover the entire field and the effective concentration may be more.

Calculation for Dilution

Commercial formulations of pesticides are generally marketed in concentrated forms, while for pest control; very low percentages of the active ingredients are required. They are thus required to be diluted before use. Along with this the total quantity of solution required to be prepared for per unit area, must also be known. Combining all of them a formula has been outlined as:

$$d = \frac{a \times b}{c}$$

where,

a: Percentage concentration of the pesticide desired.

b: Quantity of the solution/dust required for application.

c: Percentage of active ingredient available in the commercial pesticide/formulation.

d: Quantity of the commercial formulation required to be used.

For example percentage of Dimethoate solution to be used = 0.1 per cent ______(a)

Quantity of solution required to be prepared for application = 200 litres ______(b)

Percentage of active ingredient in the commercial pesticide = 30 per cent EC ______(c)

Then "d" or the quantity of the commercial pesticide required to be used will be:

$$= \frac{0.1 \times 200}{30} = 0.666 \text{ litres or } 666 \text{ ml.}$$

Weight or volume of diluent =

(quantity of solution required –
quantity of commercial pesticide required)

= (200 – 0.666) = 199.334 litres

Therefore, to obtain 200 litres of 0.1 per cent Dimethoate from Dimethoate 30 per cent EC (commercial formulation), 0.666 litre (666 ml) of Dimethoate 30 per cent EC should be added to 199.334 litres of water.

Safe Period

Since silkworms are highly sensitive to pesticides, harvest of mulberry leaves for feeding to silkworms before the safe period should be avoided. In case, if this is not followed strictly and contaminated leaves are harvested from the garden either located adjacent to field crops applied with pesticides or directly treated with pesticide, silkworm larvae develop toxic symptoms (vomiting of the digestive juice, swinging of the anterior half of the body, shortening of the body due to loss of the body fluid, paralysis etc) followed by the loss of the crop. Safe period for commonly used pesticides are presented in Table 5.1.

Application Techniques

Effective spraying or dusting are skilled jobs and hence must be planned well in advance of execution. This includes prevention of waste, uniform coverage of the target and avoiding hazards to the operator. Guidelines for effective and safe use of insecticides includes precautionary measures that have to be followed prior to application (identification of the pest, symptoms, selection of insecticide, application equipment must be kept ready, informing the neighbour farmers regarding the application programme), while

Table 5.1: Safe Periods of Other Commonly Used Pesticides

*Name of Insecticides**	*Concentration (Per cent Active Ingredients)*	*Safe Period (in days)*
Demeton (Metasystox)	0.01	11
	0.05	13
Aldrin (Aldrex)	0.01	11
	0.05	13
Phosphomidon (Dimecron)	0.01	11
	0.05	13
DDVP (Dichlorovos, Nuvan)	0.01	07
	0.05	11
Methlyparathion (Metacid)	0.01	07
	0.05	13
Carbaryl (Sevimol)	0.05	09
	0.10	11
Quinalphos (Ekalux)	0.05	07
	0.10	13
Dimethoate (Rogor)	0.05	07
	0.10	11
Endosulfan (Thiodan)	0.05	09
	0.10	17
Phosalone (Zolone)	0.05	09
	0.10	11
BHC (BHC)	0.05	07
	0.10	11
Chlordane (Termex)	0.05	11
	0.10	13
Malathion (Cythion)	0.50	13
	1.00	17

*: Names in parenthesis are the trade/commercial names of pesticides.

diluting (wearing protective devices, keeping away the children, avoid splashing while pouring the liquid solutions, never eat/drink/smoke, persons with sours and open wounds should never be allowed to carryout this work), during application (no application in the hot hours, apply dusts in early morning, don't blow clogged nozzles or hoses with mouth, under leaf coverage should be ensured) and after application (clean the equipment, destroy empty containers, keep unused pesticides safely out of the reach of children and pet animals, wash hands and body). Harvest of mulberry leaf for feeding to silkworms followed by application of insecticides should be undertaken strictly after the safe period indicated with each recommendation to avoid loss of silkworm crop due to residual toxic effect of applied insecticides. Pesticides and its formulations banned in India for use are presented in Table 5.2.

Table 5.2: List of Pesticides/Pesticide Formulations Banned in India

A. Pesticides banned for manufacture, import and use (24 Nos.)	
Aldrin	Benzene hexachloride
Calcium cyanide	Chlordane
Copper acetoarsenite	Clbromochloropropane
Endrin	Ethyl mercury chloride
Ethyl parathion	Heptachlor
Menazone	Nitrofen
Paraquat dimethyl sulphate	Pentachloro nitrobenzene
Pentachlorophenol	Sodium methane arsonate
Tetradifon	Toxafen
Aldicarb	Chlorobenzilate
Dieldrine	Maleic hydrazide
Ethylene dibromide	TCA (Trichloro acetic acid)

Contd...

Table 5.2–Contd...

B. Pesticide/pesticide formulations banned for use but their manufacture is allowed for export (3 Nos.)	
Nicotin sulphate	Phenyl mercury acelate
Captafol 80 per cent powder	
C. Pesticide formulations banned for import, manufacture and Use (4 Nos.)	
Methomyl 24 per cent L	Methomyl 12.5 per cent L
Phosphamidon 85 per cent SL	Carbofuron 50 per cent SP

Biological Control of Major Pest (Uzi fly) of Silkworm

Biological control of the pests is the most safe and eco-friendly approach in pest management strategy. In biological control, natural enemies of the pest concern those having high searching ability, synchronomous with host life, host specificity, and adaptations to field conditions, easy rearing and multiplication methods are preferred (Devanathan *et al.*, 1982). Natural parasitoids *viz.*, *Nesolynx thymus, N. dipterae, Trichopria, Exoristobia phillipinensis, Dirhinus anthracia* etc. has been identified to control Uzi fly (Kumar *et al.*, 1989; 1993a & b). So far, 20 larval/pupal parasitoids are known (Table 5.3).

Among this *N. thymus* is the most popular biological control agents of Uzi fly today, because of its high reproductive rate and higher female ratio. One lakh adult females should be released in three doses corresponding to IV and V instars and within one or two days after cocoon harvest at 8000, 16,000 and 76,000 adults respectively. Parasitoids should be released immediately after sunset in the rearing houses, places of mountage storage, near mountages with spinning larvae and also near the manure pits. However, its host searching ability and parasitization potential has kept it on the top of the other parasitoids (Table 5.4).

Table 5.3: Natural Parasitoids of Uzi Fly

Sl.No.	*Parasitoids*	*Family**	*Nature of Parasitoid***
1.	*Brachymeria intermedia*	Chalcididae	Solitary pupal
2.	*Brachymeria lugubris*	Chalcididae	Solitary pupal
3.	*Dirhinus anthracia*	Chalcididae	Solitary pupal
4.	*Dirhinus himalayanus*	Chalcididae	Solitary pupal
5.	*Exoristobia philippinensis*	Encyrtidae	Gregarious pupal
6.	*Marmoniella vitripennis*	Chalcididae	Solitary pupal
7.	*Nesolynx dipterae*	Eulophidae	Gregarious pupal
8.	*Nesolynx thymus*	Eulophidae	Gregarious pupal
9.	*Pachycrepoideus veeranai*	Pteromalidae	Solitary pupal
10.	*Pachycrepoideus vindimmae*	Pteromalidae	Solitary pupal
11.	*Pleurotropis* sp.	Pteromalidae	Solitary pupal
12.	*Spalangia cameroni*	Eulophidae	Solitary pupal
13.	*Spalangia endues*	Diapriidae	Gregarious larval
14.	*Tetrasticus howardii*	Eulophidae	Gregarious larval
15.	*Trichopriya khandalus*	Diapriidae	Gregarious larval
16.	*Trichospilus diaptraeae*	Chalcididae	Gregarious larval
17.	*Brachymeria* sp	Chalcididae	Solitary pupal
18.	*Dirhinus* sp.	Chalcididae	Solitary pupal
19.	*Trichopriya* sp.	Diapriidae	Gregarious pupal

*Order – Hymenoptera; ** Endoparasitoid.

Mass Production of *N. thymus*

N. thymus is a gregarious indigenous ecto-pupal parasitoid of Uzi fly. *N. thymus* parasitises 1–8 day old puparia of Uzi fly. Single adult female parasitises 5-6 host

Table 5.4: Searching Ability and Parasitization Potential of Parasitoids of Uzi Fly

Parasitoids	*Searching Ability (Distance in feet)*	*Parasitization Range (per cent)*
Nesolynx thymus	200	33–94
Exoristobia philippinensis	90	0–9
Trichopriya sp.	90	0–3
Dirhinus sp.	200	0–66

pupa in her life time and adults emerging from each parasitized pupae varies from 30–60. Life cycle of *N. thymus* is completed in 15–17 days. For uniform growth and development mass multiplication of the parasitoid is to be carried out at 25 ± 2°C and 60–70 per cent RH. Mass production of *N. thymus* is carried out on Uzi fly pupae or sometimes on house fly pupae. The rearing procedure is detailed by Nataraju *et al.* (2005) and furnished below:

- ☆ The Uzi fly maggots or puparia is collected from the nearest cocoon market.
- ☆ Dead maggots and melted puparia are cleaned for the purpose.
- ☆ 2–3 day old Uzi pupae (approximately 3000 in number) are spread in a single layer in an oviposition tray.
- ☆ A band of honey (50 per cent) is brushed on two paraffin paper strips and hangs in the cage through the hole provided at the top of the cage and close it with a cotton plug.
- ☆ 750 mated 2 day old well-fed females of *N. thymus* are released into the cage using a conical flask.

- ☆ Temperature of 24–26°C and relative humidity of 60–70 per cent is maintained in the cage.
- ☆ Honey in the cage is checked daily and if necessary can be added further.
- ☆ Parasitized puparia is removed on the 12th day, when the emergence of Uzi fly (if any) from un-parasitized puparia will be completed.
- ☆ Parasitized pupae are kept @300 in a single layer in one litter conical flask and the mouth of the flask is covered with muslin cloth.
- ☆ Emergence of parasitoid adults is observed.
- ☆ Paraffin paper strip with 50 per cent aqueous honey solution is provided depending on the requirement.

At 25 ± 1°C, parasitoid (*N. thymus*) emergence takes place in 15–17 days after oviposition. Generally, males emerge a few hours earlier than the females. Two days are allowed to ensure mating and feeding before collecting the parasitoid adults for field release.

Procedure for Field Release

The rationale of inundate release is that at certain periods, due to biotic and/or abiotic factors, the natural enemy population declines to a great extent, resulting in inadequate control; artificial releases during such critical periods would strengthen the population of natural enemies in abating the pest. The idea is to tilt rapidly the ratio of pest to predator in favour of the latter, thus preventing serious damage. In other words, the primary aim of inundate releases is to outnumber the pest population to bring about its immediate control without any expectations of long-term regulation, as in classical biological control. Thus, repeated releases, with the application of chemical pesticides, might be necessary. Therefore, mass production of natural enemies is an essential pre-requisite for such programmes.

(*a*) The predators are released over the entire infested area to obtain more uniform and effective control.

(*b*) Since the farmers are not familiar with handling, releasing and also the exact role of predators, it is necessary that experts should supervise the field release programme.

(*c*) The predators have to be released generally during evening hours, so that they can settle on the mealy bug colonies overnight. The required number of predators have to be assessed depending upon the area of mulberry field (Santha Kumar *et al.*, 2000).

Integrated Pest Management (IPM)

Integrated Pest Management (IPM) is a system, which utilizes all suitable pest suppression techniques in cost effective, environmental friendly and compatible manners in order to keep or maintain the pest population below those causing economic injury. The main objective of IPM is as follows:

(*a*) IPM is a broad ecological pest control approach aiming at best mix of all known pest control measures to keep the pest population below economic threshold level (ETL).

(*b*) It is an economically justified and sustainable system of crop protection that leads to maximum productivity with the least possible adverse impact on the total environment.

(*c*) It is a schedule of practices, which starts from field selection till harvest of a crop. The major components in this approach are cultural, mechanical, biological and chemical methods of insect pests, diseases, weeds etc in a compatible manner.

Central Silk Board is playing a leading role in popularisation of IPM technology among the farming sericulture community. The main activity is:

- ☆ Popularising IPM approach among farming community
- ☆ Organizing regular pest surveillance and monitoring to assess pest/disease situation and study agro-eco-system to advise timely IPM control measures
- ☆ Rearing biological control agents for their field use and conservation of naturally occurring biological control agents for control of crop pests
- ☆ Promoting use of neem based pesticides, *bacillus* based bio-pesticides, insect pathogen as alternative to chemical pesticides.
- ☆ To play a catalytic role in transfer of innovative IPM skills/methods/techniques to extension workers and farmers in all silk producing states.
- ☆ To preserve eco-system and environment;
- ☆ Human Resource Development (HRD) in IPM by imparting training to officers, extension workers and farmers
- ☆ Field releases of laboratory reared bio-control agents for the control of pests

- ☆ Issuing insect-pest and disease situation bulletins for the benefit of State functionaries and farmers

Following steps are taken in implementing the IPM technology:

- ☆ Assessment of knowledge, attitude and practice of farmers
- ☆ Identification of major pests problems responsible for low yield
- ☆ Collection and destruction of crop residues, weeds etc.
- ☆ Growing pest and disease resistant/tolerant breeds/hybrids
- ☆ Optimum spacing in rearing bed
- ☆ Use of light, yellow, sticky and pheromone traps
- ☆ Regular monitoring on pests and their natural enemies
- ☆ Conservation of crop defenders (parasites, predators and pathogens)
- ☆ Augmentation of crop defenders by release of egg, pupal, larval parasites and predators
- ☆ Use of bio-pesticides against crop pests
- ☆ Collection of egg-masses and larvae for their destruction
- ☆ Need based and judicious use of the pesticides on the basis of ETL as a last resort

IPM has been developed against the major pest (Uzi fly) of silkworm, which is summarized below:

For effective suppression of Uzi infestation, an IPM package comprising of an ovicide (uzicide–a liquid formulation of 1 per cent Benzoic acid) against eggs and augmenting release of the indigenous gregarious (*N. thymus*) and solitary (*Dirhinus* sp.) parasitoids against pupa and dusting of Dimilin on maggot/puparia to suppress the reproduction efficiency of adults has been developed (Kumar *et al.*, 1991). The package has been reported effective to suppress 77 per cent Uzi infestation. A simplified IPM package consisting of spray of uzicide and release of only *N. thymus* parasitoids has also been suggested (Kumar *et al.*, 1993a) and tested which yielded desirable result. Uzi trap as one of the component of IPM package has been suggested (Kumar *et al.*, 1996) to contain Uzi infestation effectively. However, the combination consisting of Uzicide, Uzi trap and *N. thymus* has been found to be best in containing Uzi incidence below economic injury level. It has also been demonstrated that using different combinations of management strategies (Uzicide, Uzi trap and *N. thymus*), the infestation of Uzi fly can be kept below economic injury level (5 per cent). Use of IPM package against Uzi fly has been found as the best approach in terms of eco-friendliness, higher level of pest suppression and optimization of cocoon production.

(II) DISEASE FORECASTING

Disease forecasting *i.e* the prediction of disease outbreak and its status of severity well in advance is an important measure for improving disease control decision. It also ensures appropriate control measures in preventing economic damage at the correct time for maximum effectiveness. This prediction is possible by studying the influence of biotic and abiotic environmental interference on the population of pathogen in the population of host

(Kranz, 1974). Van der Plank (1963) has formulated various equations for calculating disease epidemics in plants. These equations are used for developing forecasting models and that required accurate data on the interaction of all factors with host, pathogen and environment and their correct interpretation. Accordingly, disease assessments are made over a period of time to get reflection of disease spread. From the information obtained, infection rate (r) of pathogen is estimated to incorporate in the equation of epidemics as it fits.

(*a*) Infection Rate

Infection rate (r) of a given pathogen is calculated after determining the life cycle pattern *i.e* whether the pathogen is monocyclic or polycyclic. The monocyclic pathogens complete a part or all of its life cycle in one season. Many soil borne pathogens are in this group, and usually restricted to one generation per season. The infection rate in this case, is being calculated based on the formula as indicated below:

$$r = \frac{2.3}{t_2 - t_1} \log 10 \frac{1 - x_1}{1 - x_2}$$

where,

x_1 and x_2 are the proportion of the disease at the time t_1 and t_2 respectively.

Polycyclic pathogens, on the other hand, increase in host population logarithmically against time. Most of the foliar pathogens are in this group. Hence, the infection rate (r), which is called 'exponential infection rate' or 'apparent rate of infection', is calculated based on the assumption that the disease will multiply through several successive generations in course of an epidemic. For this the following equation can be used:

$$r = \frac{2.3\ x_2}{t_2 - t_1} \log 10 \frac{(1 - x_1)}{x_1\ (1 - x_2)}$$

where,

x_1 and x_2 are the proportions of disease at the time t_1 and t_2 respectively.

(*b*) Model for Disease Forecasting

A large number of equations have been formulated from time to time to forecast diseases in various crops, and as the time advanced, the earlier equations are modified with the use of complicated statistical methods in making perfection in forecast systems. Relatively, recently a few of the important equations are used in preparation of models for both short term and long term disease forecast separately, which can also be used effectively for disease forecasting in sericulture.

(*i*) Short-term Disease Forecast

Short term disease forecasting is done during or just before the crop season to monitor a disease during the course of growth. This requires initial status of disease or inoculum density either by calculating proportion of disease intensity or by measuring the quantum of inoculum with its infection efficiency.

(a) Forecasting Models for Monocyclic Diseases

The disease caused by monocyclic pathogen increases on the initial amount of inoculum, since, the pathogen does not produce effective inoculum during the growing season of the host. Accordingly, the forecasting can be made based on the initial disease study by using the formula indicated below:

$$x_t = x_0 rt \text{ (Fry, 1982)}$$

where,

x_t and x_0 are the proportion of disease at the time't' and '0' (initial) and 'r' is the infection rate in respect of x_t. In the other way, if the inoculum (Q) and its infection efficiency (R) are considered for the study, then 'x_0' and 'r' are to be substituted by 'Q' and 'R' respectively, and the above formula can be written as:

$$x_t = QRt \text{ (Fry, 1982)}$$

The quantum of inoculum in the above formula can be measured by counting sclerotia, spores etc., while, 'R' by the formula furnished below:

$$R = r \frac{x_t}{x_{t-p}} \text{ (Manner, 1982)}$$

where,

'p' is the latent period of infection, x_t the proportion of susceptible issue infected at time t, x_{t-p} the proportion which was infected at time t – p and which is infectious at time t, and 'r' the rate of infection in respect of x_t. Disease forecasting with the use of inoculum quantum will be very effective when climatic conditions will remain favourable all along to form an epidemic and sufficient number of hosts will be present (Shrum, 1978 and Fry, 1982).

(b) Forecasting Models for Polycyclic Diseases

Disease development by polycyclic pathogens depends on both the amount of initial inoculum and characteristic rate of exponential increase of particular pathogen (Fry, 1982). Accordingly, Van der Plank (1963) has formulated an equation for measuring an exponential growth of disease, which is being used frequently in disease forecasting. The formula is as follows:

$$x = x_0 e^{rt}$$

where,

'x' and x_0 are the proportion of the disease at time 't' and '0' (initial) respectively, 'e' the natural logarithm, as before, 'r' the apparent rate of infection and 't' the time period during which host and pathogen have to interact. Otherwise, if sporulation study is considered as the basis of forecasting the disease, then the equation developed by Blackman (1979) may be used for foliar diseases with certain modification by considering the amount of inoculum as disease intensity:

$$x = \text{In } x_0 + rt \text{ (Blackman, 1979)}$$

where,

The symbol 'In' is the natural logarithm to the base 'e' while 'x' and 'x_0' the amounts of inoculum (considered as disease intensity) at the time 't' and '0' (initial), respectively, 'r' the relative rate of sporulation and 't' the time period.

(*ii*) Long-term Disease Forecast

Long-term disease forecast, *i.e* prediction of a disease a year or several years in advance. This system does not require any study on initial disease status or quantum of inoculum like in short term. In this case disease intensity is considered as dependent variable on environmental factors. There, a relationship is established between the disease statuses and simultaneous environmental conditions *viz.,* temperature, relative humidity, rainfall, sunshine period, wind speed, dewfall etc. (as abiotic) and aphids, beetle, leafhopper, white fly etc. (biotic–vector pest), collected regularly over a long period of time to include every possible variations.

Most commonly linear regression is used for disease forecasting (Hori, 1963 and Kim, 1982). At first step, all the independent variables (abiotic factors) are analysed separately by the standard formula:

$$Y = a + bx$$

where,

'Y' (dependent variable) is the disease status in term of disease intensity, index, 'x' (independent variable) a parameter of environmental conditions and 'a' (Y-intercept) and 'b' (slope of line) the constants resulting from the observed data.

Bibliography

Abe, Y. and Fujiwara, T. (1979) Mode of multiplication of protozoan, *Pleistophora* sp. (Microsporidia – Nosematidae) in the midgut epithelium of the silkworm larvae. *J. Seric. Sci. Japan,* 48: 19-23.

Abe, H.; Kobayashi, K.; Shimada, T.; Yokoyama, T.; Maeda, S.; Hamanno, K.; Oshiki, T. and Kobayashi, M. (1993a) Infection of a susceptible/non-susceptible mosaic silkworm, *Bombyx mori* with densonucleosis virus. *J. Seric. Sci. Japan,* 62: 367-375.

Abe, H.; Shimada, T.; Kobayashi, K.; Maeda, S.; Yokoyama, T.; Oshiki, T. and Kobayashi, M. (1993b) Detection of densonucleosis virus in the silkworm, *Bombyx mori,* from faecal specimens by a polymerase chain reaction. *J. Seric. Sci. Japan,* 62: 376-381.

Alenkseenork, A. (1986) Nosematol for control of nosematosis of bees and pebrine of silkworm. *Veterinariya,* USSR, 10: 45-47.

Ananthalakshmi K.V.V.; Fujiwara, T. and Datta, R.K. (1994) First report on the isolation of three microsporidians (*Nosema* spp.) from the silkworm, *Bombyx mori* L. in India. *Indian J. Seric.*, 33: 146-148.

Anitha, T.; Shirimani; Meena, P. and Nithe Rani, R. (1994) Isolation and characterization of pathogenic bacterial species in the silkworm, *Bombyx mori* L. *Sericologia*, 34: 97-102.

Anonymous (1980) *Text Book of Tropical Sericulture*. Japan Overseas Cooperation Volunteers, Tokyo, Japan, pp. 551-556.

Ansari, M.F. and Basalingappa, S. (1987) Percent infestation of silkworm cocoons of *Bombyx mori* by the larvae of *Dermestes alter* De geer (Dermestidae: Coleoptera). *Sericologia*, 27: 587-592.

Arakawa, A. (1988) Western-blotting method for the detection of nuclear polyhedrosis virus of the silkworm, *Bombyx mori*. *J. Seric. Sci. Japan*, 57: 475-499.

Arakawa, A. (1989) Diagnosis of nuclear polyhedrosis by latex agglutination tests in the silkworm, *Bombyx mori*. *J. Seric. Sci. Japan*, 58: 257-258.

Arakawa, A. (1991) Quantitative assay of cytoplasmic polyhedrosis virus in the faeces of the silkworm, *Bombyx mori* using enzyme linked immunosorbent assay (ELISA). *J. Seric. Sci. Japan*, 60: 105-111.

Arakawa, A. and Shimizu, S. (1986) Effect of some factors on the latex agglutination test for the diagnosis of virus infectious larvae in the silkworm, *Bombyx mori*. *J. Seric. Sci. Japan*, 55: 384-387.

Arakawa, A. and Shimizu, S. (1987) Quantitative assay of densonucleosis virus of the silkworm, *Bombyx mori* by latex agglutination test. *J. Seric. Sci. Japan*, 56: 29-32.

Aruga, K. and Tanada, Y. (1971) *The Cytoplasmic Polyhedrosis Virus of the Silkworm*. University of Tokyo Press, Tokyo.

Asai, J.; Kawamoto, F. and Kawase, S. (1972) On the structure of the cytoplasmic polyhedrosis virus of the silkworm, *Bombyx mori* L. *J. Invertebr. Pathol.*, 19: 279-280.

Attathom, T. and Sinchaisri, N. (1987) Nuclear polyhedrosis virus isolated from *Bombyx mori* in Thailand. *Sericologia*, 27: 287-295.

Austrurov, B. L; Baburashvli, E. L; Bedniakova, T. A.; Vereiskaia, V. N.; Labzhanidze, V. I. and Ovanesyan, T. T. (1969) Thermal intravital disinfections of eggs with simultaneous of the embryonic diapause as a new method of control of silkworm pebrine disease. *Zvakad. Nauk., SSSR,. Ser. Bio.*, 6: 811-818.

Baig, M.; Datta, R. K.; Nataraju, B.; Samson, M. V. and Sivaprasad, V. (1992a) Protein-A linked Latex Antisera test for the detection of *Nosema bombycis* Nageli spores. *J. lnvertebr. Pathol.*, 60: 310-313.

Baig, M.; Gupta, S. K.; Nataraju, B.; Mohd Sha, M. M.; Sivaprasad, V.; Datta, R. K.; Gupta, R. and Samson, M. V. (1992b) Latex agglutination test for the detection of pebrine in the silkworm, *Bombyx mori* L. *Indian J. Seric.*, 31: 141-145.

Baig, M.; Nataraju, B. and Samson, M. V. (1990) Studies on the spread of diseases in the rearing of silkworm,

Bombyx mori L. through different sources of contamination. *Indian J. Seric.*, 29: 145-146.

Baig, M.; Samson, M. V.; Sharma, S. D.; Balavenkatasubbaiah, M.; Sashidharan, T. O. and Jolly, M. S. (1993) Efficacy of certain bed disinfectants in certain combinations against the nuclear polyhedrosis and white muscardine in the silkworm, *Bombyx mori* L. *Sericologia*, 33: 53-60.

Baig, M.; Samson, M. V.; Sashidharan, T. O.; Sharma, S. D.; Balavenkatasubbaiah, M. and Jolly, M. S. (1988a) Study on the spread of pebrine after introduction of transovarially infected worms in a colony of silkworm, *Bombyx mori* L. *Sericologia*, 28: 75-80.

Baig, M.; Samson, M. V.; Sharma, S. D.; Balvenkatasubbaiah, M.; Sashidharan, T. O. and M. S. Jolly (1988b) Effect of certain disinfectants as surface sterilants against pebrine in surface contaminated laying. *Sericologia*, 28: 81-87.

Balvenkatasubbiah, M.; Ananthalakshmi, K.V.V.; Selvakumar, T.; Nataraju, B. and Datta, R.K. (1999) Chlorine dioxide, a new disinfectant in sericulture. *Indian J. Seric.*, 38: 125-130.

Balvenkatasubbiah, M.; Datta, R. K.; Baig, M.; Nataraju, B. and lyengar, M. N. S. (1994) Efficacy of bleaching powder as a disinfectant against the pathogens of silkworm, *Bombyx mori* L. *Indian J. Seric.*, 33 : 23-26.

Balvenkatasubbiah, M.; Nataraju, B. and Datta, R.K. (1996) Chlorine dioxide and Virkon-S as disinfectant against pathogens of silkworm, *Bombyx mori* L. *Indian J. Seric.*, 35: 50-53.

Balvenkatasubbiah, M.; Nataraju, B.; Baig, M. and Datta, R.K. (1994) Comparative efficacy of different disinfectants against nuclear polyhedrosis virus (*Bm*NPV) and *Beauveria bassina* of silkworm, *Bombyx mori* L. *Indian J. Seric.*, 33: 142-145.

Barman, A. C.; Pasha, K. and Nahar, A. (1990) Study on the control of Uzi fly, *Tricholyga bombycis* (Beck.) in silkworm, *Bombyx mori* L. *Bull. Seric. Res.*, 1: 65-69.

Batra, R. C. and Sinha, M.K. (1971) A fungal parasite of Plum hairy caterpillar, *Euproctis fraternal* Moore (Lepidoptera: Lymantriidae). *Labdev. J. Sci. Tech.*, 9-B: 228-229.

Battu, G. S.; Bindra, O. S. and Rangarajan, M. (1971) Investigations on microbial infections of insect pests in Punjab. *Indian J. Entomol.*, 33: 317-325.

Bedniakova, T. A. and Vereiskaia, V. N. (1958) The disinfection action of high temperature on eggs on mulberry silkworm (*B. mori* L) infected with Pebrine (*N. bombycis*) at different stages of the diapausal cycle of development (in Russian). *Doklady Akad. Nauk, USSR, Biol. Sci. Sect.*, 122: 760-763.

Bhat, K. P. (1986) Laboratory studies on the Indian Uzi fly, *Exorista sorbillans* (Wiedemann) (Diptera: Tachinidae) and its management. M. Sc. (Agric.), Thesis, UAS, Bangalore, p. 103.

Bhattacharya, J.; Krishnan, N.; Chandra, A. K.; Prakash, O. and Sengupta, K. (1993) Use of slide agglutination test for the detection of nuclear polyhedrosis virus of silkworm, *Bombyx mori* L. *Current Science*, 65: 638-639.

Bhattacharya, S. S.; Chakraborthy, N. and Sahakundu, A. K. (1993) Effect of bleaching powder solution as ovicide against Uzi fly, *Exorista sorbillans*; in *'Recent Adv. Uzi fly Res'*, Channabasavanna, G. P.; Veeranna, G. and Dandin, S. B. (eds.), pp. 191-200.

Blackman, V. H. (1979) The compound interest law and plant growth. *Ann. Bot.* (London), 33: 353-360.

Byrareddy, M. S.; Devaiah, M. C.; Narayanaswamy, T. K.; Govindan, R. and Shyamala, M. B. (1991) Comparative efficacy of some rearing tray disinfectants in prevention of silkworm white muscardine caused by *Beauveria bassina* (Bales). *Sericologia*, 31: 533-535.

Canning, E.U.; Curry, A.; Cheney, S.A.; Lafranchi-Tristem, N.J.; Kawakami, Y.; Hatakeyama, Y.; Iwano, H. and Ishihara, R. (1999) *Nosema tyriae* and *Nosema* sp., Microsporidian Parasites of cinnabar moth *Tyria jacobaeae. J. Invertebr. Pathol.*, 74: 29-38.

Carlos, A.; Didier,.P and Jean, C. (1996) Recovery and characterization of a replicas complex in rotavirus-infected cells by using a monoclonal antibody against NSP2. *J. Virol.*, 70: 985-991.

Chandra, A. K. and Sahakundu, A. K. (1993) The effect of drug on pebrine infection in *Bombyx mori* L. *Indian J. Seric.*, 31 & 32: 67-69.

Channabasavanna, G. P.; Siddappaji, C. and Dandin, S. B. (1993) Integrated management of Indian Uzi fly, *Exorista bombycis* infesting the mulberry silkworm. *Rec. Adv. Uzi-fly Res., Proc. Natl. Sem. Uzi fly and its Control*, KSSRDI, Bangalore, pp. 227-237.

Chen, C. (1988) Detection of densonuleosis virus of *Bombyx mori*. *Canye Kexue*, 13: 201.

Chen, J.; Teng, J.; Hu, C. and Michael, M. (1989) Production of monoclonal antibodies to densovirus of silkworm (*Bombyx mori*) and their application in diagnosis. *Chinese J. Virol.*, 5: 77-81.

Cheng, L.J. and Hou, R. F. (1992) Factors enhancing *Bombyx mori* nuclear polyhedrosis virus infection in-vitro. *J. Appl. Ento.*, 113: 103-106.

Cheung, W.W.K. and Wang, J.B. (1995) Electron microscopic studies on *Nosema mesnili* (Microsporidia: Nosematidae) infecting the malpighian tubules of *Pieris canidia* larva. *Protoplasma*, 186: 142-148.

Chinnaswamy, K. P. and Devaiah, M. C. (1984) Susceptibility of different races of silkworm, *Bombyx mori* L. to *Aspergillosis*. *Sericologia*, 24: 513-517.

Chinnaswamy, K. P. and Devaiah, M. C. (1986) Studies on the control of *Aspergillosis* of the silkworm, *Bombyx mori* L. *Indian J. Seric.*, 25: 63-69.

Chitra, C.; Karanth, N.G.K. and Vasantharajan, V.N. (1975) Diseases of the mulberry silkworm, *Bombyx mori* L. *J. Sci. Indust. Res.*, 34: 386-401.

Chowdhary, S.N. (1967) *The Silkworm and its Culture*. Mysore Printing and Publishing House, Mysore, India, pp. 76.

Dasgupta, K. P. (1962) Observations on behavior of Uzi fly maggots. *Indian J. Seric.*, 2: 16-18.

Datta, R. K. (1992) Integrated Pest Management (IPM) – an answer to Uzi menace. *Indian Silk*, 30: 36-37

Datta, R. K. and Mukherjee, P. K. (1975) Control of the silkworm pest, *Tricholyga bombycis*. II. Mating competitiveness of chemosterilized and normal males. *Chemosterilant News*, 3: 16-20.

Datta, R. K. and Mukherjee, P. K. (1978a) Life history of *Tricholyga bombycis* (Diptera: Tachinidae) a parasite of *Bombyx mori* L. (Lepidoptera: Bombycidae). *Ann. Ent. Soc. America*, 71: 767-770.

Datta, R. K. and Mukherjee, P. K. (1978b) Sterilization of *Tricholyga bombycis*, a parasite of *Bombyx mori* with tepa and thiotepa. *J. Econ. Ent.*, 71: 373-376.

Devaiah, M. C. and Krishnaswami, S. (1975) Observations on the seasonal incidence of pebrine disease of the silkworm, *Bombyx mori* L. *Indian J. Seric.*, 14: 27-30.

Devaiah, M. C. and Patil, G. M. (1986) Indian Uzi fly and its management; in *'Lectures on Sericulture'*, Boraiah, G. (ed.), Bangalore University, pp. 123-125.

Devaiah, M. C.; Rajashekharagowda, R. and Chinnaswamy, K. P. (1983) A new fungal pathogen *Aspergillus nidulans* on the eri silkworm, *Samia cynthia ricini* (Lepidoptera: Saturniidae). *Indian J. Seric.*, 21 & 22: 71-72

Devanathan, P. H.; Kasturi Bai, A. R. and Ranganathan, V. S. (1982) Biological control of Uzi fly. *Current Science*, 51: 1120-1121.

Dychdala, G.R. (1983) Chlorine and chlorine compounds; in *'Disinfection, Sterilization and Preservation'*, Block, S. S. (ed.), Lea and Febiger, Philadelphia, USA. pp. 157-182.

Enomoto, S.; Moriyama, H. and Iwanami, S. (1987) *Septicemia* occurrence in cocoons as related to silkworm rearing conditions. *J.A.R.Q.*, 21:117-121.

Flora, C.A.M.; Samson, M.V.; Nataraju, B.; Balvenkatasubbaiah, M. and Datta, R.K. (1996) Progressive histopathological changes in nuclear polyhedrosis virus infected tissues of the silkworm, *Bombyx mori* L. *Sericologia*, 36: 227-236.

Fry, W. E. (1982) *Principles of Plant Disease Management*. Academic Press, New York.

Fujiwara, T. (1979) Infectivity and pathogenecity of *Nosema bombycis* to larvae of the silkworm. *J. Seric. Sci. Japan*, 48: 376-380.

Fujiwara, T. (1980) Three microsporidians (*Nosema* spp.) from silkworm *Bombyx mori*. *J.Seric. Sci. Japan*, 49: 229-236.

Fujiwara, T. (1984a) A *Pleistophora* – like microsporidian isolated from the silkworm, *Bombyx mori*. *J. Seric. Sci. Japan*, 53: 398-402.

Fujiwara, T. (1984b) *Thelohania* sp. (Microsporidia–Thelohanidae) isolated from the silkworm, *Bombyx mori*. *J. Seric. Sci. Japan*, 53: 459-460.

Fujiwara, T. (1993) Comprehensive report on the silkworm disease control. A report on *"Bivoltine Sericulture Technology Development in India"* submitted to Central Silk Board, Bangalore, India, pp.110.

Fujiwara, T. (1985) Microsporidia from silk moths in egg production sericulture. *J. Seric. Sci. Japan*, 54: 108-111.

Fujiwara, T. and Kagawa T. (1984) Control of *Nosema bombycis* parasitizing silkworm eggs by treatment with hydrochloric acid on exposure to various temperatures. *J. Seric. Sci. Japan,* 53: 394-397.

Geethabai, M.; Patil, C. S. and Kasturi Bai, A. R. (1985) A new method for easy detection of pebrine spores. *Sericologia,* 25: 297-300.

Gochnaner, A. and Margetts, P. (1980) A microsporidian disease in the silkworm, *Bombyx mori* L. *Sericologia,* 33: 201-210.

Gorpade and Kumar, D. (1986) Identity of *Exorista* species (Diptera: Tachinidae) parasites in mulberry silkworm, *Bombyx mori* (Lepidoptera: Bombycidae) in India. *Colomania,* 2: 55-56.

Govindan, R.; Narayanaswamy, T. K. and Devaiah, M. C. (1998) *Principles of Silkworm Pathology*. Seri Scientific Publishers, Bangalore, India, pp.422.

Govindan, R.; Veeresh, G. K.; Shyamala, M. B.; Devaiah, M. C:; Narayanaswamy, T. K. and Sasthry, M. N. (1990) Effect of simultaneous infection of silkworm, *Bombyx mori* L. with Kenchu virus and *Straphytococcus aureus* Rosenbach. *Indian J. Seric.,* 29: 273-278.

Govindaraju, R. and Saratchandra, S. (1984) A few observations on the host parasite interaction between the Uzi fly, *Exorista sorbillans* (Wiedemann) (Diptera: Tachinidae) and its hosts, *Bombyx mori* L. (Lepidoptera: Bombycidae). *Entomol. Exp. Appl.,* 36: 61-68.

Grobov, O. F. and Rodionova, Z. E. (1985) Identification of spores of *Nosema bombycis* from silkworm. *Veterinarira,* Moscow, USSR, 12: 70-71.

Guerine-Meneville (1849) cit. in Pebrine disease of silkworm, a technical report, Tatsuke, K. (ed) (1971), Overseas Technical Co-operation Agency, Tokyo, Japan.

Guo, X. J.; Qiwan, Y. J. and Hu, X. F. (1985a) The diagnosis of the densonucleosis disease of the silkworm (*Bombyx mori*) in the early stage of infection by immuno-peroxidase histochemical method. *Scientia Agricultura Sinica*, 8: 82-85.

Guo, X. J.; Qiwan, Y. J.; Hu, X. F. and Wang, H. L. (1985b) Studies on the infection site of the densonucleosis virus in the diseased silkworm (*Bombyx mori* L.) in China. *Canye Kexue*, 11: 93-98.

Gupta, B. K.; Mistri, P. K.; Ghosh, M. G. and Chakraborthy, S. (1988) Mass killing of Uzi maggots by stifling of silkworm, *Bombyx mori* L. *Indian Silk*, 26: 55-56.

Han, M. S. and Watanabe, H. (1987) Immunoperoxidase-staining method for discrimination of microsporidian spores in the pebrine infection of silkworm mother moths. *J. Seric. Sci. Japan*, 56: 431-435.

Han, M. S. and Watanabe, H. (1988) Transovarian transmission of two microsporidia in the silkworm, *Bombyx mori* and disease occurrence in the progeny population. *J. Invertebr. Pathol.*, 51: 41-45.

Han, M. S.; Nguyen, M. T. and Lim, J. S. (1997) Establishment of simplistic moth inspection system to prevent *Nosema bombycis* infection of the silkworm, *Bombyx mori*. *Korean J. Seric. Sci.*, 36: 69-75.

Hashimoto, Y.; Watanabe, A. and Sironmani, A. (1997) Detection of *Nosema bombycis* infection in the silkworm, *Bombyx mori* by Western blot analysis. *Sericologia*, 39: 209-216.

Hatakeyama, Y. and Hayasaka, S. (2001) Specific amplification of microsporidia DNA fragments using multi-primer PCR. *J. Seric. Sci. Japan*, 70: 163-166.

Hayasaka, S. (1990) Inhibitory effect of high temperature on the development of *Nosema bombycis* in the silkworm, *Bombyx mori. Acta Seri. Entomol.*, 3: 59-65.

Hayasaka, S. and Ayuzawa, C. (1987) Diagnosis of microsporidians, *Nosema bombycis* and closely related species by antibody-sensitized latex. *J. Seric. Sci. Japan*, 56: 169-170.

Hitoshi, I. and Ishihara, R. (1981) Inhibitory effect of several chemicals against the hatch of *Nosema bombycis* spores. *J. Seric. Sci. Japan*, 50: 276-281.

Hou, R.F. and Chang, J. (1991) Cellular defense response to *Beauveria bassinna* in the silkworm, *Bombyx mori. Appl. Entomol. Zool.*, 20: 118-125.

Hukuhara, T. (1985) 'Pathology associated with cytoplasmic polyhedrosis virus'; in *'Viral Insecticides for Biological Control'*, Maramorosch, K. and Sherman, K.E. (eds.), pp. 121-162, Academic press, New York.

Ishihara, R. (1963) Effect of injection of *Nosema bombycis* (Nageli) on pupal development of the silkworm, *Bombyx mori* L. *J. Insect Pathol.*, 5: 131-140.

Ishihara, R. and Iwano, H. (1991) The lawn grass cutworm, *Spodoptera depravata* (Butter) as a natural reservoir of *Nosema bombycis* Nageli. *J. Seric. Sci. Japan*, 60: 236-337.

Ito, T; Hukahara, T. and Akami, K. (1985) Improved method of detection of polyhedra of cytoplasmic polyhedrosis virus recovered from silkworm faeces. *J. Seric. Sci. Japan*, 54: 1-5.

Iwano, H. and Ishihara, R. (1981) Inhibitions effect of several chemicals against hatching of *Nosema bombycis* spores. *J. Seric. Sci. Japan*, 50: 276-281.

Iwashita, Y. (1971) Histopathology of cytoplasmic polyhedrosis; in *'The Cytoplasmic Polyhedrosis Virus of the Silkworm'*, Aruga, H. and Tanada, Y. (eds.), pp. 79-102, University Tokyo Press, Tokyo.

Iwashita, Y. and Zhou, C.D. (1988) Inactivation by treatment of a nuclear polyhedrosis virus of the silkworm, *Bombyx mori* L. with calcium hydroxide solution. *J. Seric. Sci. Japan*, 57: 511-518.

Jolly, M. S. (1981) *Uzi fly, its identification, prevention and control*. CSR&TI, Mysore, Bull. No. 4, p. 8.

Jolly, M. S. (1982) Uzi fly incidence and its preventive measures. *Reshme Krishi*, 4: 27-32.

Jolly, M. S. (1986) *Pebrine and its Control*. Central Silk Board, publication, Bangalore, India.

Jolly, M. S. and Kumar, P. (1985) A three pronged approach to control Uzi fly. *Indian Silk*, 23: 5-9.

Jolly, M. S.; Baig, M. and Chandrasekharaiah (1982) Silkworm rearing under nylon net–a short-term control measure evolved by CSR&TI, Mysore. *Workshop on Uzi fly Control*, CSR&TI, Mysore, 7-8.

Kagawa, T. (1980) The efficacy of formalin as disinfectant of *Nosema bombycis* spores. *J. Seric. Sci. Japan*, 49:218-222.

Kasturibai, A. R.; Mahadevappa, D.; Nirmala, M. R., and Jyothi, H. K. (1986) Control of Uzi fly by semiochemicals. *Curr. Sci.*, 55: 1038.–1040

Kawarabata, T. and Hayasaka, S. (1987) An enzyme-linked immunosorbent assay to detect alkali-soluble spore surface antigens of strains of *Nosema bombycis* (Microspora: Nosematidae). *J. Invertebr. Pathol.*, 50: 118-123.

Kawarabata, T. (2003) Review – Biology of microsporidians infecting the silkworm, *Bombyx mori* in Japan. *Insect Biochemistry & Sericology*, 72: 1-32.

Kawase, S. and Kurstak, E. (1990) Parvoviridae of invertebrates; in *Virus of invertebrates* (Ed. E. Kurustak), Academic Press, New York, 315-343.

Ke, Z.; Xie, W.; Wabg, X.; Long, Q. and Pu, Z. (1990) A monoclonal antibody to *Nosema bombycis* and its use for identification of microsporidian spores. *J. Invertebr. Pathol.*, 56: 395-400.

Kishore, S.; Baig, M.; Nataraju, B.; Balavenkatasubbaiah, M.; Sivaprasad, D.; Iyengar, M.N.S. and Datta, R.K. (1994) Cross infectivity of microsporidians isolated from wild lepidopteron insects to silkworm, *Bombyx mori* L. *Indian J. Seric.*, 33: 126-130.

Kobayashi, H. (1992) Spread and prevention of NPV. *Science and Technology*, 31: 40-42.

Kobayashi, H. and Yamazaki, D. (1987) Discrimination of microsporidian spores with fluorescent antibody techniques in the insects. *Gunma J. Agric. Res. – Series B.*, 4: 25-28.

Kobayashi, M. and Chaeychomsri, S. (1993) Thermal inhibition of viral diseases in the silkworm, *Bombyx mori* L. *Indian J. Seric.*, 32: 1-7.

Kobayashi, M.; Inagaki, S. and Kawase, S. (1981) Effect of temperature on the development of nuclear polyhedrosis virus in the silkworm, *Bombyx mori*. *J. Invertebr. Pathol.*, 38: 386-394.

Kotikal, Y. K.; Reddy, D. N. R. and Subbrayudu, B. V. (1989) Netting the tray covers is an ideal approach for Uzi management. *Indian Silk*, 28: 33-34.

Kramer, J.P. (1976) The extra corporal ecology of microsporidia; in *Comprehensive Pathology*. Bulla L.A. and Cheng, L.A. (eds.), Vol. I. Pp. 127-135, Plenum Press, Publishing Corporation, New York.

Kranj, J. (1974) The role and scope of mathematical analysis and modeling in epidemiology; in "*Epidermis of Plant Disease: Mathematical Analysis and Modelling*, J. Kranz (ed.) pp. 7-54, Springer-Verlag, Berlin and New York.

Krishnaswamy, S.; Narasimhanna, M. N.; Suryanarayan, S. R. and Kumararaj, S. (1973) *Sericulture Manual–2. Silkworm Rearing*, FAO, Agricultural Services Bulletin, 15/3, Rome, Italy.

Kumar, A.; Kumar, P.; Singh, B. D.; Noamani, M. K. R. and Sengupta, K. (1989) Biological control of Uzi fly through parasites. *Indian Silk*, 27: 25.

Kumar, P. (1987) Contribution to our knowledge on *Tricholyga bombycis*, a serious parasite of *Bombyx mori* and its control. Ph. D. Thesis, Mysore University, Mysore, p. 328.

Kumar, P., Jayaprakash, C. A.; Kishor, R. and Sengupta, K. (1990) Effect of gamma radiation on the reproductive potential of Uzi fly. *Indian J. Seric.*, 29: 295-296.

Kumar, P. and Jolly, M. S. (1986a) Seasonal effect of certain developmental stages of *Tricholyga bombycis* Beck (Diptera: Tachinidae). *Proc. Indian Acad. Sci. (Anim. Sci.)*, 25: 561-566

Kumar, P. and Jolly, M. S. (1986b) Efficacy of nylon net enclosure in containing Uzi fly (*Tricholyga bombycis*) infestation to silkworm (*Bombyx mori* L.). *Indian J. Seric.*, 25: 74-77.

Kumar, P.; Jolly, M. S.; Datta, R.K., Samson, M.V. and Reddy, V.V. (1985) Studies on reduction of infestation by Uzi fly, *Tricholyga bombycis* (Beck) on pre-spinning and spinning silkworm, *Bombyx mori* L. with chemical dusting. *Indian J. Seric.*, 24: 53-57.

Kumar, P.; Jolly, M. S. and Sharma, S. D. (1987) Uzicide–a new product of universal applicability to contain Uzi fly. *Indian Silk*, 25: 13-15.

Kumar, P.; Kishor, R.; Girdhar, K. and Sengupta, K. (1993) Observations on some ethological aspects of Uzi fly, a parasitoid of mulberry silkworm. *Mysore J. Agric. Sci.*, 27: 154-159.

Kumar, P.; Manjunath, D.; Prasad, K. S. and Datta, R. K. (1991) Integrated pest management, a successful tool to suppress Uzi menace in sericulture. *IV. Natl. Symp. Growth Dev. Control Tech Insect Pests*. U.P. Zoological Society, Muzaffaenagar, p. 69.

Kumar, P.; Manjunath, D.; Kumar, V.; Katiyar, R. L.; Prasad, K. S.; Kishor, R.; Narayanaswamy, K. C. and Datta, R. K. (1996) New trap to contain Uzi fly. *Indian Silk*, 36: 13-15.

Kumar, P.; Manjunath, D. and Datta, R. K. (1993a) Biological control of Uzi fly. *Proc. Natl. Semi. Uzi fly and its Control*, KSSRDI, Bangalore, pp. 91-106.

Kumar, P.; Prasad, K. S.; Kishore, R.; Manjunath, D. and Datta, R. K. (1993b) Efficacy of introduced indigenous parasitoid against Uzi fly, *Exorista sorbillans*. *Proc. Natl. Semi. Uzi fly and its Control*. KSSRDI, Bangalore, pp. 127-133.

Kumar, V.; Kumar, P.; Katiyar, R. L. and Datta, R. K. (1995) Bleaching powder – a novel agent for pest management. *Indian Silk*, 33: 23-25.

Kumar, V.; Kumar, P. and Manjunath, D. (1993) Gross external morphology of embryo of *Exorista sorbillans* (Diptera: Tachinidae). *Rec. Adv. Uzi fly Res*. pp. 79-89.

Kurisu, K. (1986) Simplified calculation of the operating characteristics in the pebrine inspection of the grouping mother method. *J. Seric. Sci. Japan*, 55: 351-352.

Kurisu, K.; Nakasone, S.; Dohi, M. and M. Hamazaki (1985) Studies on the pebrine inspection of the mother moth in the silkworm, *Bombyx mori* for commercial eggs. III. Practical application of sampling inspection table. *Bull. Fac. Text. Sci., Kyoto Univ.*, 11: 19-30.

Li, D. (1985) Studies on the serological diagnosis of the pebrine of silkworm, *Bombyx mori*, by slide agglutination test. *Sci. Seric.*, 11: 99 -102.

Liu, S.X. (1984) A summary of the techniques for the control of *Nosema bombycis* in *Bombyx mori* with instant acid treatment at high temperature. *Guangdong Agric. Sci.*, 3: 20-21.

Liu, S. X. and Xhong, W. B. (1989) The research channels in the prevention and control of silkworm diseases. *Sericologia*, 29: 287-295.

Maeda, S. and Watanabe, H. (1978) Immunofluorescence observation of the infection of densonucleosis virus in the silkworm, *Bombyx mori*. *Jap. J. Appl. Entomol. Zool.*, 22: 98-101.

Malone, L.A. and Mclvor, C.A. (1995) DNA probes for two microsporidia, *Nosema bombycis* and *Nosema costelytrae*. *J. Invertebr. Pathol.*, 65: 269-273.

Malone, L.A.; Broadwell, A.H.; Lindridge, E.T.; McIvor, C.A. and Ninham, J.A. (1994) Ribosomal RNA genes of two microsporidia, *Nosema apis* and *Vavraia oncoperae*, are very variable. *J. Invertebr. Pathol.*, 64:151-152.

Manners, J. G. (1982) *Principles of Plant Pathology*. Cambridge University Press, Cambridge, London.

Matsumoto, T.; Yafeng-Zhu and Kazuhiko, K. (1985) Mixed infections with flacherie virus and bacteria in *Bombyx mori*. *J. Seric. Sci. Japan*, 54: 453-456.

Mathur, B. N.; Singh, V. and Sharma, S. K. (1970) Occurrence of parasitic *Aspergillus fumigatus* (Free) on *Utethesis pulchella* L. (Arctiidae: Lepidoptera) in Rajasthan. *Indian J. Ent*, 32: 393-394.

Mattews, R. E. F. (1982) Classification and nomenclature of viruses. *Intervirology*, 17:1-5.

Mei, L. and Jin, W. (1998) Study on distinguishing *Nosema bombycis* by SPA co-agglutination. *Sci. Seric.*, 14: 110-111.

Mike, A.; Ohmura, H.; Ohwaki, M. and Fukuda, T. (1989) A practical technique for pebrine inspection by microsporidian spore specific monoclonal antibody sensitized latex. *J. Seric. Sci. Japan*, 58: 392-395.

Mike, A.; Ohwaki, M.; Fukuda, T. and Miyahara, S. (1984) Preparation of monoclonal antibodies to the *Bombyx mori* cytoplasmic polyhedrosis virus. *J. Seric. Sci. Japan*, 53: 59-63.

Miyajima, S. (1981) Application of some serological reaction of silkworm viruses by use of blood sampling paper. *Res. Bull. Aichi-Ken Agric. Res. Centre*, 13: 293-296.

Miyajima, S. and Kawase, S. (1968) Effect of high temperature on the incidence of cytoplasmic polyhedrosis of silkworm, *Bombyx mori* L. *J. Seric. Sci. Japan*, 37: 390-394.

Miyamoto, K. (1989) The detection of spores of *Nosema bombycis* (Microspora: Nosematidae) by enzyme immunoassay. *Acta Sericologia Entomologica*, 1: 11-20.

Müller, A.; Trammer, T.; Chioralia, G.; Seitz, H.M.; Diehl, V. and Franzen, C. (2000) Ribosomal RNA of *Nosema algerae* and phylogenetic relationship to other microsporidia. *Parasitol. Res.*, 86: 18-23.

Nagamine, T.; Kobayashi, M.; Saga, S. and Hoshimo, M. (1991) Preparation and characterization of monoclonal antibodies against occluded virions of *Bombyx mori* nuclear polyhedrosis virus. *J. Invertebr. Pathol.*, 57: 311-324.

Nageswararao, S.; Muthulakshmi, M.; Kanginakudru, S. and Nagaraju, J. (2004) Phylogenetic relationships of three new microsporidians isolated from the silkworm, *Bombyx mori*. *J. Invertebr. Pathol.*, 86: 87-95.

Nageswararao, S.; Surendranath, B. and Saratchandra, B. (2005) Characterization and phylogenetic relationships among microsporidia infecting silkworm, *Bombyx mori*, using inter simple sequence repeat (ISSR) and small subunit rRNA (SSU-rRNA) sequence analysis. *Genome*, 48: 355-366.

Nair, R. R. and Premkumar, T. (1974) *Aspergillus flavus* Link, a parasite on the leaf eating caterpillar, *Lymantria obfuscata* Wlk. *Current Science*, 45: 563.

Nakagaki, M.; Takei, R. and Nagashima, E. (1987) Improved method of purification of infectious flacherie virus and *Bombyx* densonucleosis virus. *J. Seric. Sci. Japan*, 56: 338-342.

Narayanaswamy, K. C. (1991) Population dynamics of Indian Uzi fly, *Exorista bombycis* (Louis) (Diptera: Tachinidae). *Ph.D. Thesis, UAS, Bangalore*, pp. 223.

Narayanaswamy, K. C. and Devaiah, M. C. (1994) The development of life tables of Uzi fly, *Exorista bombycis* (Louis) (Diptera: Tachinidae). *Indian J. Ecol.*, 21: 45-49.

Narayanaswamy, K. C. and Devaiah, M. C. (1998) *Silkworm Uzi fly*. Zen Publishers, Bangalore, p. 232.

Narayanaswamy, K. C. and Devaiah, M. C. (1999) An overview on silkworm Uzi fly; in *Advances in Mulberry Sericulture*. Devaiah, M. C.; Narayanaswamy, K. C. and Maribashetty, V. G. (eds.), CVG Publications, Bangalore, pp. 475-497.

Narayanaswamy, K. C.; Devaiah, M. C. and Govindan, R. (1993a) Bioecology of Indian Uzi fly, *Exorista bombycis* (Louis) (Diptera: Tachinidae). *Bull. Seric. Res.*, 4: 27-31.

Narayanaswamy, K. C.; Devaiah, M. C. and Govindan, R. (1993b) Field incidence and biology of Uzi fly, *Exorista bombycis* (Louis) of two noctuid species. *Geobios*, 20: 250-254.

Narayanaswamy, K. C.; Devaiah, M. C. and Govindan, R. (1993c) Ovipositional behavior of Uzi fly, *Exorista bombycis*. *Proc. Natl. Sem. Uzi fly and its Control*, KSSRDI, Bangalore, pp. 43-48.

Narayanaswamy, K. C.; Devaiah, M. C. and Govindan, R. (1993d) Studies on the life tables of Uzi fly, *Exorista bombycis*. *Proc. Natl. Sem. Uzi fly and its Control*, KSSRDI, Bangalore, pp. 31-42.

Narayanaswamy, K. C.; Devaiah, M. C. and Govindan, R. (1994a) Mating behavior of Uzi fly, *Exorista bombycis* (Louis) (Diptera: Tachinidae), a parasitoid of silkworm, *Bombyx mori* L. *Ann. Entomol.*, 12: 37-43.

Narayanaswamy, K. C.; Devaiah, M. C. and Govindan, R. (1994b) Mating behavior of Uzi fly, *Exorista bombycis* (Louis) (Diptera: Tachinidae), a parasitoid of silkworm, *Bombyx mori* L. *Proc. Natl. Acad. Sci. India*, 64 (B): 257-262.

Nataraju, B. (1995) Studies on diagnosis and prevention of nuclear polyhedrosis in silkworm, *Bombyx mori* L. Ph.D. Thesis, University of Mysore, India.

Nataraju, B., Baig, M., Balavenkatasubbaiah, M., Venkatareddy, S., Singh, B. D. and Noamani, M. K. R. (1993) Comparative toxicity and infectivity titer of *Bacillus thuringiensis* to silkworm, *Bombyx mori* L. *Indian J. Seric.*, 32 : 103-105.

Nataraju, B., Balavenkatasubbaiah, M., Baig, M., Singh, B. D. and Sengupta, K. (1991) A report on the distribution of *Bacillus thuringiensis* in Sericultural areas of Karnataka. *Indian J. Seric.*, 30: 56-58.

Nataraju, B., Balavenkatasubbaiah, M.; Sharma, S.D.; Selvakumar, T.; Thiagarajan, V. and Datta, R.K. (2002) A practical technology for diagnosis and management of diseases in silkworm rearing. *Int. J. Indust. Entomol.*, 4: 169-173.

Nataraju, B. and Datta, R.K. (1999) Application of textile dye based dipstick immunodiagnostic kit for management of infectious flacherie in silkworm rearing. *Proc. XVII International Sericultural Commission Congress, Egypt*, pp. 283-288.

Nataraju, B., Datta, R. K. Baig, M., Balavenkatasubbaiah, M.; Samson, M. V. and Sivaprasad, B. (1998). Studies on the prevalence of nuclear polyhedrosis in sericultural areas of Karnataka. *Indian J. Seric.*, 37: 154-158.

Nataraju, B.; Datta, R.K.; Sivaprasad, B. and Baig, M. (1994a) Protein-A linked latex antisera (PALLAS) test for the detection of nuclear polyhedrosis in silkworm, *Bombyx mori* L. *Indian J. Seric.*, 33: 27-33.

Nataraju, B.; Datta, R.K.; Sivaprasad, B.; Gupta, S.K. and Shamin, M. (1994b) Colloidal textile dye based dipstick immunoassay for the detection of nuclear polyhedrosis virus (BmNPV) of the silkworm, *Bombyx mori* L. *Invertebr. Pathol.*, 63: 135-139.

Nataraju, B.; Sivaprasad, B. and Datta, R.K. (1999) Studies on the cause of 'Thatte Roga' in silkworm, *Bombyx mori* L. *Indian J. Seric.*, 38: 149-151.

Nataraju, B.; Sivaprasad, B. and Datta, R.K. (2002) Studies on the development of an oral 'Vaccine' against nuclear polyhedrosis in silkworm, *Bombyx mori* L. *Sericologia,* 40: 421-427.

Nataraju, B.; Sathyaprasad, K.; Manjunath, D. and Aswani Kumar, C. (2005) *Silkworm Crop Protection.* Central Silk Board Publication, Bangalore, India, pp. 412.

Nitta, M. and Watanabe, H. (1984) Effect of formalin on characterization of nuclear polyhedrosis of the silkworm, *Bombyx mori* L. *J. Seric. Sci. Japan,* 53: 146-150.

Oblisami, G.; Ramamoorthi, K. and Rangaswamy, G. (1969) Studies on the pathology of some crop pests of South India. *Mysore J. Agric. Sci.,* 3: 86-98.

Ovanesyan, T.T. and Lobzhanidze, V.I. (1960) First results of experiments on thermal disinfection on pebrinous silkworm eggs by a brief immersion in hot water. *Inst Mortl Zhivotnykh Akad Nauk SSSR,* 21: 184-215.

Patil, C. S. (1989) New record of fungal pathogen *Aspergillus flavus* (Link) on mulberry silkworm, *Bombyx mori* L. from India. *Current Science,* 58: 683.

Patil, C. S. (1991) Studies on the evaluation of calcium hydroxide against cytoplasmic polyhedrosis of the silkworm, *Bombyx mori* L. *Entomon,* 16: 147-150.

Patil, C. S. (1993) Review on pebrine–a microsporidian disease in the silkworm, *Bombyx mori* L. *Sericologia,* 33: 201-210.

Patil, C. S. and Geethabai, M. (1985) *Guidelines for identification of pebrine spores in grainages*, KSSRDI publication, Bangalore, India.

Patil, C. S. and Geethabai, M. (1989) Studies on the susceptibility of silkworm races to pebrine spores. *J. Appl. Entomol.*, 108: 421-423.

Patil, C. S.; Jyothi, N. B. and Dass, C. M. S. (2001) Silkworm faecal pellets examination as diagnostic method for detecting pebrine. *Indian Silk*, 39: 11-12.

Patil, G. M. (1983) Investigations on the Uzi fly, *Exorista sorbillans* (Wiedemann) (Diptera: Tachinidae) infesting silkworm, *Bombyx mori* (L). M. Sc. (Agri.) Thesis, UAS, Bangalore, p. 104.

Patil, G. M. and Govindan, R. (1984a) Biology of Uzi fly, *Exorista sorbillans* (Widemann) (Diptera: Tachinidae). *Indian J. Seric.*, 23: 22-31.

Patil, G. M. and Govindan, R. (1984b) Effect of temperature on the development of Uzi fly, *Exorista sorbillans* (Widemann) (Diptera: Tachinidae) in silkworm *Bombyx mori* L. *Indian J. Seric.*, 23: 38-41.

Persoons, C. J.; Veeranna, G.; Vos, J. D. and Nagasundara, K. R. (1993) The role of semio-chemicals in the host finding behavior of parasites, with special reference to the Uzi fly, *Exorista sorbillans. Proc. Natl. Sem. Uzi fly and its Control*, KSSRDI, Bangalore, pp. 167-189.

Peter, A.; Sadatulla, F. and Devaiah, M.C. (1999) The viral, bacterial and protozoan diseases of the silkworm, *Bombyx mori* L.; in *Advances in Mulberry Sericulture*, Devaiah, M.C.; Narayanaswamy, K.C. and Maribashetty, V.G. (eds), pp. 378-457, C.V.G. Publications, Bangalore, India.

Prasad, N.R. (1990) Contribution to the pathology of silkworm, *Bombyx mori* L. infested with endoparasite

Uzi fly, *Exorista sorbillans*. Ph.D. Thesis, University of Mysore, India.

Quadrefague, A. De. (1860) cit. in Pebrine diseases of silkworms–a technical report, Tatsuke, K. (1971) Overseas Technical Co-operation Agency, Tokyo, Japan.

Ratna S.; Nataraju, B.; Selvakumar, T.; Chandrasekharan, K. and Thiagarajan, V. (2003) Relationship between the susceptibility of silkworm, *Bombyx mori* to densonucleosis and infectious flacherie virus infection. *Indian J. Seric.*, 42: 10-25.

Samson, M.V. (2000) Cocoon production and silkworm protection. *National Conference on Strategies for Sericulture Research & Development*, 16-18 November, CSR&TI Mysore, India, pp. 38-48.

Samson, M. V.; Baig, M.; Sapru, M. L. and Narasimhanna, M. N. (1986) Efficacy of certain fungicides and disinfectants for the control of white muscardine disease in mulberry silkworms. *Indian J. Seric.*, 23: 78-83.

Samson, M. V.; Santha, P. C.; Singh, R. N. and Sashidharan, T. O. (1999a) A new microsporidian infecting *Bombyx mori* L. *Indian Silk*, 37: 10-12.

Samson, M. V.; Santha, P. C.; Singh, R. N. and Sashidharan, T. O. (1999b) Microsporidian spore isolated from *Pieris* sp. *Indian Silk*, 38: 5-8

Santha, P.C.; Sashidharan, T.O.; Singh, R.N.; Daniel, A.G.K. and Veeraiah, T.M. (2001) Identification of intermediary stages of *Nosema bombycis* for diagnosis of pebrine–a new approach. *Indian Silk*, 40: 13-14.

Sashidharan, T. O.; Singh, R. N.; Samson, M. V.; Manjula, A.; Santha, P. C. and Chandrashekharaiah (1994)

Spore replication rate of *Nosema bombycis* (Microsporidia: Nosematidae) in the silkworm, *Bombyx mori* L. in relation to pupal development and age of moths. *Insect Sci. Applic.*, 15: 427-431.

Sato, R. and Watanabe, H. (1980) Purification of mature microsporidian spores by isodensity equilibrium centrifugation. *J. Seric. Sci. Japan*, 49: 512-516.

Sato, R. and Watanabe, H. (1986) Pathways of oral infection with four microsporidae in the silkworm, *Bombyx mori* L. *J. Seric. Sci. Japan*, 55:10-26.

Sato, R.; Kobayashi, M.; Watanabe, H. and Fujiwara, T. (1981) Serological discrimination of several kinds of microsporidian spores isolated from the silkworm, *Bombyx mori* by an insect fluorescent antibody test. *J. Seric. Sci. Japan*, 50: 180-184.

Sato, R.; Shimizu, T. and Inoue, H. (1978) Immunofluorescence observation on the small flacherie virus antigen in the silkworm, *Bombyx mori* infected with an Ina-isolate virus. *J. Seric. Sci. Japan*, 47: 175-176.

Sato, R.; Masahiko, K.; Watanabe, H. and Fujiwara, T. (1982) Serological discrimination of several kinds of microsporidian spores isolated from the silkworm, *Bombyx mori* L., by an indirect fluorescent antibody technique. *J. Invertebr. Pathol.*, 40: 260-265.

Saxena, K. D. and Rawatt, R. R. (1968) Bionomics of *Drosicha mangiferae* (Green) on citrus including new record of its three natural enemies. *Madras Agric. J.*, 55: 309-313.

Selvakumar, T.; Nataraju, B. and Datta, R.K. (1999) Characterization of *Bacillus thuringiensis* varieties in relation to pathogenicity to silkworm, *Bombyx mori*. *Indian J. Seric.*; 38: 75-78.

Seki, H. (1986) Effects of physiochemical treatments on a silkworm densonucleosis virus of the silkworm, *Bombyx mori*. *Appl. Ent. Zool.*, 21: 515-518..

Seki, M. and Sekijima, Y. (1976) Detection of the specific antigen of the infectious flacherie virus in the silkworm, *Bombyx mori* by single radial immunodiffusion method. *J. Seric. Sci. Japan*, 45: 13-18.

Sengupta, K.; Kumar, P.; Baig, M. and Govindaiah (1990) *Handbook on pest and disease control of mulberry and silkworm*. Economics and Social Commission for Asia and Pacific, United Nations, Bangkok, Thailand.

Sheeba, R.; Devaiah, M.C.; Chinaswamy, K.P. and Govindan, R. (1999) Thermotherapy of pebrinized cocoons and its effect on larval progeny; in *Proc. Natl. Semi. Trop. Seri.* Govindan R, Chinaswamy K.P, Krishnaprasad N.K, Reddy D.N.R. (eds), Vol. II., pp. 266-272, UAS and Swiss Agency for Development and Cooperation, Bangalore, India.

Shi, L. and Ding, H. (1989) Studies on the detection of densonucleosis virus using biotin-avidin system (BAS) in the silkworm, *Bombyx mori*. *Sericologia*, 29: 371-377.

Shi, L. and Jin, P. (1997) Study on the differential diagnosis of *Nosema bombycis* of the silkworm, *Bombyx mori* by monoclonal antibody-sensitized latex. *Sericologia*, 37: 1-6.

Shimizu, S. (1982) Enzyme-linked immunosorbent assay for the detection of flacherie virus of the silkworm, *Bombyx mori. J. Seric. Sci. Japan*, 51: 370-373.

Shimizu, S. and Arakawa, A. (1986) Latex agglutination test for the detection of cytoplasmic polyhedrosis virus and the densonucleosis virus of the silkworm, *Bombyx mori. J. Seric. Sci. Japan*, 55: 153-157.

Shimizu, S.; Ohba, M.; Kanda, K. and Aizawa, K. (1983) Latex agglutination test for the detection of the flacherie virus of the silkworm, *Bombyx mori. J. Invertebr. Pathol.*, 42: 151-155.

Shimizu, S.; Tauchi, S. and Arakawa, A. (1991) Protein A–coated latex linked antisera test for the detection of densonucleosis virus of the silkworm, *Bombyx mori. J. Invertebr. Pathol.*, 57: 124-125.

Shiva Prasad, V.; Nataraju, B.; Renu, S. and Datta, R.K. (2003a) Colloidal textile dye-based dipstick immunoassay for the detection of infectious flacherie of silkworm, *Bombyx mori* L. *Int. J. Indust. Entomol.*, 6: 27-31.

Shiva Prasad, V.; Nataraju, B.; Baig, M.; Samson, M.V. and Datta, R.K. (2003b) ELISA for the detection of nuclear polyhedrosis virus of silkworm, *Bombyx mori* L. *Int. J. Indust. Entomol.*, 6: 179-181.

Shiva Prasad, V.; Renu, S.; Nataraju, B. and Datta, R.K. (1997) Protein-A linked antisera test for detection of infectious flacherie virus. *Indian J. Expt. Biol.*, 35: 1203-1207.

Shrum, R. D. (1978) Forecasting of epidermis; in *"Plant Pathology: An Advanced Treatise"*, Horshfall, J. G. and

Cowling, E. B. (eds.) Vol. 2, pp.223-238, Academic Press, New York.

Siddappaji, C. (1985) Bioecology and management of Indian Uzi fly, *Exorista sorbillans* (W.) (Diptera: Tachinidae) a parasite of mulberry silkworm. Ph.D. Thesis, UAS, Bangalore, pp. 163.

Siddappaji, C. and Channabasavanna, G. P. (1981) Silkworm Uzi fly and its management. *Krishivarthe*, 6: 19-22.

Siddappaji, C. and Channabasavanna, G. P. (1990) The Indian Uzi fly, *Exorista bombycis*, a parasitoid of mulberry silkworm. *Indian J. Seric.*, 29: 129-137.

Siddappaji, C. and Channabasavanna, G. P. (1992) External structure of the Indian Uzi fly, *Exorista bombycis* (Diptera: Tachinidae) a parasitoid of mulberry silkworm. *Mysore J. Agric. Sci.*, 26: 289-303.

Singh, R.N.; Daniel, A.G.K.; Sindaggi, S.S. and Kamble, C.K. (2007) Microsporidians infecting silkworm, *Bombyx mori*. *Sericologia*, 47: 1-16.

Singh, R. N.; Maheswari M. and Saratchandra, B. (2004) Sampling, surveillance and forecasting of insect population for integrated pest management in sericulture. *Intl. J. Indust. Entomol.*, 8: 17–26.

Singh, R. N.; Yadav, P. R. and Singh, T. (1992) Containing the pebrine problem in sericulture. *Indian Silk*, 30: 43–44.

Singh, T. and Saratchandra, B. (2003) Microsporidian disease of the silkworm, *Bombyx mori* L. (Lepidoptera: Bombycidae). *Intl. J. Indust. Entomol.* (Korea), 6: 1-9.

Singh, T. and Saratchandra, B. (2004) *Principles and Techniques of Silkworm Seed Production*. Discovery Publishing House, New Delhi, pp. 362.

Singh, T.; Bhat, M.M. and Khan, M.A. (2010) *Silkworm Egg Science: Principles and Protocols*. Daya Publishing House, New Delhi, pp. 276.

Singhamony, I. A.; Chandrakala, T. S. and Jamil, K. (1990) A novel agar-based food attractant for Uzi fly, *Exorista sorbillans*. *Curr. Sci.*, 59: 609-610.

Sironmani, A. (1997) Detection of *Nosema bombycis* infection in the silkworm, *Bombyx mori* by Western blot analysis. *Sericologia*, 39: 209-216.

Smyk, D. (1959) Methodes physiques de lutte contre *Nosema bombycis* dans les graines du ver a soie du murier. *Revue du Ver a Soie.*, 11: 155-164.

Sprague, V. (1982) *Microspora;* in *Synopsis and Classification of Living Organism*. Parker, S.P. (ed.), Vol. 1, pp.589-594, McGraw Hill Book Co., New York.

Srikanta, H. K. (1986) Studies on the cross infectivity and viability of *Nosema bombycis* (Microsporidia: Nosematidae). M. Sc. Thesis UAS Bangalore, India, pp. 106.

Talukdar, J. N. (1980) Prevalence of transovarian infection of microsporidian parasite infecting muga silkworm, *Antheraea assamensis*. *J. Invertebr. Pathol.*, 36: 273-275.

Tatsuke, K. (1971) Pebrine disease in silkworms. *A Technical Report*, Overseas Technical Cooperation Agency, Tokyo, Japan.

Tau, K.; Nishimori, K.; Miyamoto, K. and Yamakawa, M. (1990) Inhibitory effect of monoclonal antibodies against *Bombyx mori* nuclear polyhedrosis virus on virion adherence by mid-gut cells. *VIII International Congress on Virology*, Berlin, West Germany, pp. 155.

Thangavelu, K. and Sahu, A. K. (1982) A note on the phenomenon of population regulation in Uzi fly (*Exorista sorbillans* Wied) (Diptera: Tachinidae). *Natl. Acad. Sci. Let.*, 5: 359-360.

Thangavelu, K. and Sahu, A. K. (1986) Some studies on the bionomics of *Exorista sorbillans* (Wied.) from North Eastern India. *Sericologia*, 26: 77-82.

Thiagarajan, V. and Govindaiah (1987) Menace of dermestid beetles in grainages. *Indian Silk*, 26: 26-27.

Tian, G. and Max, M. (1996) The destructive effect of chlorine dioxide on pathogens of silkworm, *Bombyx mori*. *J. Annui. Agric. Univ.* (China), 23: 525-538.

Vander Plank, J. E. (1963) *Plant Diseases: Epidermis and Control*. Academic Press, New York.

Vavra, J. and Maddox, J.V. (1976) Methods in microsporidiology; in *Comparative Pathobiology*. Bulla, L.A. and Cheng, T.C. (eds.), Vol. I., pp. 107-121, Plenum Publishing Corporation, New York.

Veber, J. (1958) A comparative histopathology of the microsporidians, *Nosema bombycis* on different hosts; in *Transactions of the First International Congress of Insect Pathology and Biological Control*, pp. 301-314, Praha.

Veeranna, G. and Nirmala, M.R. (1989) Courtship and mating behavior of the Uzi fly, *Tricholyga bombycis* Beck. (Diptera: Tachinidae). *Entomon*, 14: 85-89.

Venkatareddy, S.; Singh, B. D.; Baig, M.; Sengupta, K.; Giridhar, R. and Singhal, B. K. (1990) Efficacy of asiphor as a disinfectant against incidence of diseases of silkworm, *Bombyx mori. Indian J. Seric.*, 29: 147-148.

Vijay, Veer Negi, B.K. and Rao, K.M. (1996) Dermestid beetles and some other insect pests associated with stored silkworm cocoons in India, including a world list of Dermestid species found attacking this commodity. *J. Stored Prod. Res.*, 32: 69-89.

Virendrakumar; Nataraju, B.; Thiagarajan, V. and Datta, R.K. (2002) Application of systemic fungicide for control of white muscardine in silkworm, *Bombyx mori* L. *Int. J. Indust. Entomol.*, 5: 171-174.

Virendrakumar; Nataraju, B.; Thiagarajan, V. and Dandin, S.B. (2003) Influence of systemic fungicide on the hematology of silkworm, *Bombyx mori* L. infected with *Beauveria bassinna. Int. J. Indust. Entomol.*, 6: 11-14.

Vossbrink, C. B.; Maddox, J. V.; Friedman, S.; Debrunner-Vossbrink, B. A. and Woese, C. R. (1987) Ribosomal RNA sequence suggests Microsporidians are extremely ancient eukaryotes. *Nature*, 326: 411-414.

Wang, Y. X.; Ma, J. Y.; Pan, H. H.; Zou, F. Z. and Mou, Z. H. (1988) Epidemiological study of a densonucleosis virus in *Bombyx mori. Canye Kexue*, 14: 25-29.

Watanabe, H. (1971) Resistance of the silkworm to cytoplasmic polyhedrosis virus; in *'The Cytoplasmic polyhedrosis virus of the silkworm'*, Aruga, H. and Tanada, Y. (eds.), 169-184.

Watanabe, H. (1981) Characteristics of densonucleosis in the silkworm, *Bombyx mori. J.A.R.Q.*, 15: 133-136.

Watanabe, H. (2002) Genetic resistance of the silkworm, *Bombyx mori* to viral diseases. *Current Science*, 83: 439-446.

Weiser, J. (1969) Immunity of insects to protozoan; in *Insects Immunity to Parasitic Animals*. Jackson, C.J.; Herman, R. and Singer, I. (eds.), pp. 129-147, Appleton Century Crofts, New York.

Weiser, J. (1977) Contribution to the classification of microsporidia. *Vestn Cask Spol Zool.*, 41: 308-321.

Index

C

D

Y